The COURIER
is proud to present the
ARIZONA TERRITORIAL COOKBOOK
by Melissa Ruffner Weiner
(with Budge Ruffner) as part of the
COURIER'S 100th anniversary celebration.

Frontier lifestyles are captured within these pages
through authentic recipes, personal accounts,
and photographs passed down from the very people
who struggled first to carve out a life in Arizona
and then struggled to make it better.

Looking back over a century of existence,
the COURIER greatly appreciates the influence
and heritage of the past. We dedicate this book
to the people of Arizona and to the people of
Yavapai County, whose courage, ingenuity, and
perserverance established the foundation for
Arizona's future.

the courier

Serving Prescott
and Central Yavapai
County Since 1882

Johnny Hovey, son of Sheriff Hovey of Graham County — born in Clifton, Arizona Territory on June 17, 1889. Photograph courtesy of Sharlot Hall Museum

ARIZONA TERRITORIAL COOKBOOK
The Food and Lifestyles of a Frontier

Melissa Ruffner Weiner
with Budge Ruffner

Donning Company/Publishers
Norfolk/Virginia Beach

Other regional and specialty cookbooks in the Donning series include: *Savannah Sampler* by Margaret Wayt DeBolt, *The Great Chicago Melting Pot Cookbook* by Agnes Feeney and John Leckel, *The Ham Book: A Comprehensive Guide to Ham Cookery* by Monette R. Harrell and Robert W. Harrell, Jr., *New Life Cookbook* (based on the health and nutritional philosophy of Edgar Cayce) by Marceline Newton, *The Sacramento Cookery Book* by Sally A. Clifford, *The Legendary Illinois Cookbook* by Agnes Feeney and John Leckel, and *Norfolk Cookery Book* by Sandy Kytle Woodward.

*This book is lovingly dedicated to our friends
Lois, Charles, Sharlot, Nellie,
Josephine, Gail, Helen, and Elisabeth;
their knowledge spans a century,
and in their wisdom, they have preserved
the past for the present.*

"A man's real possession is his memory. In nothing else is he rich, in nothing else is he poor."

— Alexander Smith

Prescott Public Library, built in 1903, showing the interior as it originally looked. Photograph from author's collection

Contents

"Many of these wonderful human documents I have found written out by the shaking hands of our old pioneers; men whose hands were more used to holding the rifle, or the pick and drill, or the reins of a cow horse, or the handles of a plow, than a pen. . . .For many years I have dreamed of seeing these things published for our own Arizona people, for our young people growing up, for the strangers who come to us and ask to know the real life of Arizona."

From
Cactus and Pine by Sharlot
M. Hall 2nd Edition, Arizona
Republican Print Shop
(Phoenix) 1924

Placer miner. Photograph courtesy of the Department of Library, Archives and Public Records, State of Arizona

Foreword

ARIZONA TERRITORIAL COOKBOOK: THE FOOD AND LIFESTYLES OF A FRONTIER is refreshing in its subject of the Arizona frontier woman and her ambience, a topic that has not been equitably noted by most writers of Western life.

Melissa Ruffner Weiner, and her father, co-author Budge Ruffner, are descendants of one of Yavapai County's first families and qualified by lineage and by their appreciation of Arizona's heritage to give us a look at our past. In embracing this bit of Americana, they have presented an important legacy to us and to our posterity.

History has slighted the role of the woman in her influence and contribution to the development of the frontier. Writers have recorded man's eminence: his courage, hardships, achievements. Artists (men and women) depicting early times have generally focused on the man, the Indian, the animal. When have you seen a sculpture of a frontier woman and her work in bronze? Yet, the woman was one-half of the family. She had to pull her own weight in the primitive land; this need and duty brought out a new democratic woman, giving her a freedom and elevation seldom attained by her Eastern sisters. This breed of woman should be acknowledged. Her life and times have been portrayed by Mrs. Weiner who has unearthed never-before-printed materials and photographs.

"An army travels on its stomach" is attributed to Napoleon. "The way to a man's heart is through his stomach" is advice given to maidens since the nineteenth century. Another aphorism in Western vernacular could be stated: "The West was won — by its grub." The woman and her vittles were a mainstay in conquering the country.

Mrs. Weiner's cookbook is comprised of recipes from these frontier cooks. Preserved with the original spelling and punctuation, these voices of the past lend color, flavor, and authenticity to the text. Mrs. Weiner has included pertinent material and photographs to illuminate the background which enhances and clarifies our understanding. We see the beauty and the ugliness of the country, the serenity and the violence of the times. We empathize with the people in their joys and sorrows, in their failures and successes. We are lifted and relieved with the inclusion of the humor. By these details we can relate the frontier woman to her environment.

Dedicated to accuracy, the authors have portrayed a valuable and needed chapter to our frontier Arizona. Being in complete harmony with these ideals and purpose, I am proud to be honored by adding my comments to this exciting and worthwhile project.

Marguerite Noble

Marguerite Noble was born in 1910 in Gila County in the Arizona Territory where her parents were "in the cow business." Formerly a school teacher in Phoenix, she is now retired in Payson, Arizona. Her first novel *Filaree* deals with a ranch woman's evolution in pioneer times in the West, and has been optioned by CBS for television.

Introduction

The recipes which appear in this publication were carefully selected from a variety of sources, including: cook books popular between the 1860s and 1912; recipes contributed by descendants friends and family who assisted in locating information on specific dishes; early newspapers; personal diaries and letters; and menus of the time. The scrapbooks of Nellie von Gerichten Smith, provided by Helen Hartin of Hartin's Red Door Antiques, have been particularly important as a source of recipes, home remedies, natural cosmetics, household hints, and background information of the 1880s and 1890s. All journal and diary entries, personal letters, and newspaper excerpts which appear in quotes include spelling and punctuation as originally written.

Although it has been necessary to adapt some recipes to include more readily available ingredients, or to do without more specific cooking instructions, these recipes, remedies, and photographs reflect individual lifestyles in three cultures as they existed in Arizona during territorial days. Some recipes are printed exactly as found, and information on yield, exact kind or quantity of ingredients and/or baking time or temperature is not specific enough to guarantee good results. Because they are an equally important part of our heritage, we continue to try to recreate these dishes and encourage the more adventuresome to do so, as well.

Please bear in mind that these foods were prepared in a variety of altitudes, from 138 feet at Arizona City (later Fort Yuma) to 6,905 feet at Flagstaff. A number of these recipes have been used by Prescott families or tested in our mile-high altitude. As women of the frontier found, cooking at levels below 2,500 feet or above 6,000 feet may require some persistence. Many dishes will need no adjustment, but if you find it necessary the following ideas may prove helpful:

Liquids with moisture-holding properties, such as sour milk, buttermilk and cream are not usually part of recipes prepared at lower elevations. However, if any of these ingredients are called for, increase liquid 2 to 3 tablespoons per cup for over 6,000 feet; decrease about 2 tablespoons for 2,500 to 4,000 feet.

To convert a recipe for use at altitudes over 4,000 feet you should increase the amount of flour by about 2 teaspoons for every cup called for. For sugar and shortening, decrease 1 to 2 tablespoons per cup — 3 tablespoons per cup for over 6,000 feet.

Increase baking powder, soda or cream of tartar ¼ to ½ teaspoon from 2,500 to 4,000 feet; over 6,000 feet, decrease ¼ to ½ teaspoon.

Note: Adjust your leavening ingredient first. You may find that it is not necessary to adjust other components of the recipe, but this can only be discovered by trial and error.

Baking temperature should be decreased 10 to 20 degrees for 2,500 to 4,000 feet; increased by 20 degrees for over 6,000 feet. Watch your cooking time carefully. Some foods will take less time to cook at higher elevations because of low humidity and more rapid evaporation. Other dishes may take longer than usual.

We suggest preparing a new recipe in small quantity until you know from experience what results you will obtain at your altitude.

The story of life in the Arizona Territory is as diverse as the many different voices which tell it. Although space and time limitations made it impossible for us to relate every experience or portray each culture completely, perhaps in these pages you will find forgotten memories and a feeling of kinship; or change your view of life on the great Western frontier, seeing it not as Hollywood has represented it but as it really was. Hopefully you will understand more fully the people and appreciate their enormous sacrifices and tenacious belief in the future of this wild and untamed land.

We have strived to permanently record representations of territorial lifestyles so that they will not be forgotten. It is our hope that you will not only find them historically significant, but that they will also enhance your greater appreciation of the contributions of past generations to present-day life.

Pottery shards dating from 1150 A.D. give substantial evidence that the Hopi village of Oraibi, on the high desert of Northern Arizona, is today the oldest continuously inhabited community in the United States.

This is Mishongnovi, one of the six Hopi pueblos then existing. On the ladder leading up to the second and third floors stands a woman, the owner of the house. On the terraces of the upper tiers, corn and meat have been put out to dry; on the walls hang nets of red chilis, and here and there sit pouches and household utensils; a large earthen water-jar, wrapped in a blanket, was drenched frequently with water to cool the contents by evaporation (a method later used by the pioneers.) The chimneys were made of bottomless earthen pots placed upside down, one on the other, and the joints cemented with mud.

On the roof of the pueblos was often a large, loosely-built cage where captured eagles were kept for the sake of their feathers which, like those of the turkey, were largely used in the dresses and headpieces worn by the ceremonial dancers. Photograph courtesy of the Department of Library, Archives and Public Records, State of Arizona

12

Native Peoples

When Francisco Vasquez de Coronado and his conquistadores entered Arizona in 1540, many of the area's 250,000 Indians were growing crops. In the southern section of Arizona, the Pimas and Papagos were and still are the best farmers. Cultivating the arid land with little water, they grew beans, corn, melons, squash, tomatoes, fruits, and berries. The saguaro fruit which grows on top of the giant cactus was harvested and consumed by both the Pimas and Papagos then as it is today. This event was so important to their life cycle that it marked the beginning of their year. The Hopi, living in northern Arizona on rock-capped mesas surrounded by high desert, grew corn, beans, melons, squash, pumpkins, peaches, and maize. What they could not produce they did without, raiding and stealing being against their principles. Not so with the Navajo and Apache. Many of their material needs were met by raiding other tribes or Mexican villages in Sonora. Hunting, however, supplied food for all seventeen of Arizona's Indian tribes; rabbit, deer, and wild turkey were the favorites.

Prior to the arrival of Father Eusebio Francisco Kino in 1691, what few fish there were in the streams of Arizona were prized protein for all but the Navajos who refused to eat creatures of the water, believing them to be reincarnated ancestors returned to life in aquatic form. Father Kino introduced cattle, sheep, horses, wheat, and European fruits and vegetables to the Indians which added to the variety of the native diet. For three centuries, the Spanish occupied what we today call the Southwest, followed by a brief Mexican period, which lasted only about twenty-five years.

The war with Mexico in 1848 and the Gadsden Purchase of 1854 established the boundaries of the New Mexico Territory, of which Arizona was then the western portion. This new frontier afforded unlimited opportunity and settlers began to pour into the area.

When the sixth territorial governor of Arizona visited Boston in 1883, he was the honored guest of Governor Bullock of the Great Commonwealth of Massachusetts at a festive dinner. Governor Frederick A. Tritle was somewhat annoyed as he listened to the assembled dignitaries sing the praises of the advanced society of Massachusetts as compared to the primitive frontier of Arizona. During the course of that elegant evening, one of the guests raised his glistening goblet to Governor Bullock and suggested a toast to the governor of the "oldest commonwealth." Governor Tritle of Arizona seized the opportunity and responded. He thanked the proper Bostonians for the honor accorded him as governor of Arizona. He reminded them that Arizona had a school ably conducted by missionaries long before Harvard had set out its first sprigs of ivy. He called their attention to an order of government and civilization centuries old; the ancient acumen necessary to construct a vast system of irrigation canals was cited; Arizona's heritage of Spanish law, he mentioned, was well established long before the first tea leaves struck the chilled surface of Boston harbor. It was an educational experience, a history lesson, which now, a century later, is all too frequently forgotten.

Corn Meal Cakes
(Adapted)

These were often made with blue Indian cornmeal as that color has religious significance to many tribes. Whole wheat flour may be substituted for blue cornmeal and used in the same quantity.

Yield: 16 to 20 medium-sized pancakes

2½ cups blue cornmeal
3 teaspoons baking powder
½ teaspoon salt
2 tablespoons sugar

5 tablespoons shortening, melted
3 or 4 eggs
1¾ cups milk

Combine the first four ingredients in a large mixing bowl. Add shortening, eggs, and milk. Mix well. Spoon on to a slightly greased griddle, turning once as cakes brown. Serve hot with honey, jelly, or cinnamon and sugar.

Corn meal cakes were later prepared in much the same way by the pioneers, but because they were cooked on a hoe propped in front of the fire, they were called hoe cakes.

These Hopi maidens are grinding corn on a metate using a mano. The cornmeal will probably be used for household cooking although other cornmeal was used by Hopi priests during their annual snake dance and other religious rituals.

This stereopticon view, taken in 1903, shows the ceremonial hairdo worn only by unmarried girls. The coils, made in the shape of a squash blossom, are wound over the ends of wooden hoops and then tied tightly. Their necklaces repeat the squash blossom design, which represents fertility in nature. The crescent at the bottom was copied from the naja, an old-world amulet worn on the forehead bridle piece of the conquistadores' steeds to ward off the evil eye.

The walls of the room are decorated with evergreen boughs intertwined with "kitchen" Kachinas, storage pots line a high shelf, and ceremonial sashes and horse cinches hang above the man sitting on a sheep skin. Photograph courtesy of Sharlot Hall Museum

15

Hoe Cakes

Yield: 12 to 16 medium-sized hoe cakes

2 cups cornmeal
1 teaspoon salt
2 tablespoons lard (shortening)

1 cup hot water
1 cup cold water, approximately

Mix the cornmeal, salt, and lard in a bowl. Add hot water and stir well. Thin with cold water to pouring consistency. Drop on a hot griddle, turning once. Serve crisp and hot with honey, jelly, or cinnamon and sugar.

This Hopi woman is making a bread very similar to the Mexican tortilla. The rounds are individually cooked over a small fire and then cooled and served in the coiled baskets seen in the foreground. For hundreds of years, the Hopi used coal as a fuel because of its abundance in their area. Photograph courtesy of the Department of Library, Archives and Public Records, State of Arizona.

Fry Bread

(Adapted)

Yield: 10 to 12 medium-sized bread rounds

4 cups white flour
5 teaspoons baking powder
1½ teaspoons salt

2 to 2¼ cups warm water
Dry milk as needed
Shortening for frying

Mix the flour, baking powder, and salt in a large bowl. Gradually stir in water to make a soft sticky dough. Continue stirring until the dough is smooth and elastic; adding a little dry milk will keep it from sticking to the sides of the bowl, and it will rise more. Cover the bowl with a clean towel and set it aside for 30 minutes. Then shape dough into balls about the size of an apricot. If the dough sticks to your fingers, use dry milk instead of more flour to roll the dough in because flour discolors the grease. The dry milk adds protein and the texture of the fry bread is improved. Pat the dough back and forth by hand until it becomes larger and thinner; the more you work it, the better it will be. Be sure to leave one small hole in the finished dough to let the evil spirits out.

Put shortening into a heavy skillet at least one inch deep and heat until it bubbles when dough is placed in it. If you add a piece of raw potato, it prevents the pan from burning and keeps the fat at the same heat. Place the dough gently in the hot fat so it won't spatter. Turn the fry bread with a long-handled fork when it becomes puffy and is a golden brown on one side. After the other side is brown too, place the fry bread on absorbent paper. This is best when eaten warm and you can serve it in a variety of ways:

Roll it in cinnamon and sugar, or confectioners' sugar.

Cook apple, peach, or berry filling in dough which has been pinched closed with your fingers, or serve the filling on top.

Serve with honey.

Cover the fry bread with any combination of beans, lettuce, tomatoes, cheese, onions, chilis, and meat.

Prickly Pear Jelly I
(Adapted)

2½ cups apple juice
1 cup prickly pear juice
½ cup lemon juice

1 package pectin
5½ cups sugar

Mix apple, prickly pear, and lemon juices together with one package of pectin. Cook to a rolling boil, stirring constantly. Add the sugar slowly, continuing to stir while mixture boils for five minutes. Skim off the foam and pour carefully into sterilized jars. Seal with paraffin.

— Carmen Villarreal Hamilton

Prickly Pear Jelly II
Yield: About 6 medium jars

Prickly pear fruit, about 2 dozen pieces
Water, as needed

1 tablespoon pectin
3 tablespoons lemon juice
3½ cups sugar

Collect the pears when they are dark red; usually they ripen in late August, September, and early October. Be sure to use tongs or heavy gloves and don't eat any of the fruit you collect because of the thorns. Put fruit in cold water and some of the stickers will come off, then hold with tongs and scrub each piece under cold running water. Fill a pan with enough water to cover the fruit and bring to a boil. Add the fruit and blanch it for about 30 seconds, just a few pieces at a time so that the fruit can be peeled as soon as it begins to cool. After the outer skin is removed, slice the fruit in half and remove all seeds. Break up the seed clusters and retrieve as much of the pulp as possible and add this to the seedless fruit. Mash the fruit pulp as finely as possible and then strain it through a strainer lined with a double thickness of cheesecloth to catch any overlooked stickers or seeds. Two dozen pieces of fruit should yield about 1 quart of juice.

Measure 2½ cups of the fruit juice and combine in a saucepan with 1 tablespoon pectin. Bring to a fast boil, stirring constantly, and add lemon juice and sugar. Boil for 3 minutes and immediately remove from the burner. Skim off the foam, fill sterilized jars, and seal with hot paraffin.

Note: Cacti are protected under the Arizona law, so don't disturb the plant, just gather and enjoy its natural bounty.

Banana Yucca Pie
(Adapted)

The ripe fruit of the Banana Yucca (a member of the lily family) is pulpy and sweet tasting, somewhat like pineapple. It is at its peak in mid-summer and can be eaten raw, roasted, dried, or ground into meal. Despite its odd name, the results of this recipe are really quite tasty.

⅓ to ¾ cups sugar, depending on the sweetness of the fruit
½ teaspoon each of cinnamon and nutmeg
2 teaspoons cornstarch
½ teaspoon salt
3 to 4 tablespoons butter

2 egg yolks
½ teaspoon vanilla extract
½ cup thick cream
4 to 6 cups diced raw fruit of the yucca, enough to fill a pie
Pastry crust, unbaked

Mix dry ingredients and add to butter creamed with egg yolks and vanilla. Add cream slowly, stirring constantly to avoid lumps, then fold in fruit. Spoon mixture into the pie crust. Top with second crust and slit top in several places. Brush with butter or egg whites and bake at 350 degrees F. for 45 minutes or until golden brown.

Note: If yucca is out-of-season or not available in your area, substitute two parts sliced apples and one part raisins.

There are thirty varieties of yucca and virtually every part of the plant has usefulness to the Indian. The fruit, seeds, and petals provide nourishment, medicine, and dye. Fibers and leaves are used to make baskets, mats, rope, cloth, sandals, brooms, and toys. Roots of the "soapweed" (*Yucca Baccata*) are pounded and the pulp used as soap and shampoo, not only for personal hygiene but also in rituals surrounding birth, puberty, marriage, and death.

These Yavapai Indian women are enjoying a moment of relaxation while caring for the little papoose, who is understandably the center of attention. The cradleboard in which the baby is carried has been laid on the ground near the door of the family's house, or wikieup. These shelters were constructed of tree branches or bushes and covered with deer hides, canvas, or cloth. The basket on the ground to the right of the entrance is covered with pitch to make it waterproof. In this way, dry camps could be supplied with water for cooking, drinking, and other daily use. Photograph courtesy of Sharlot Hall Museum

Wild Grape Jelly
(Adapted)

This is just like jelly from purchased grapes except for the first — and best — part.

Yield: depends on number of grapes cooked

Gather grapes, slightly underripe, being careful to save some for the pot. Wash and cull out unripened or bad berries. Remove stems. Cover berries with water in a large kettle, cooking them slowly to soften. Press through a colander or cheesecloth to separate pulp from seeds and skins. Return pulp to kettle and add an equal amount of sugar. Cook the mixture slowly for about 40 to 45 minutes, stirring occasionally. Pour into sterilized canning jars and seal.

Lucy Miller, third daughter of Yavapai Chieftess Viola Jimulla, explains that the closest thing to an Indian recipe was the oral instructions and traditions passed down in a family. Foods were gathered according to their season and prepared simply for immediate use or preserved and put away for future needs. Nevertheless, there were some foods which were particularly enjoyed. The fresh juice of the saguaro cactus was very similar to grape juice, but the Yavapai did not have to accept the substitute because wild grapes were abundant, especially around Point of Rocks (now Granite Dells). Wild grapes were eaten fresh, dried, and boiled into a sweet jelly-like mixture. By 1881 Tom and James Wing were homesteading the area and began cultivating domestic grapevines.

Mutton or Lamb Stew

Yield: 6 to 8 servings

3 roasted green chilies (or one per person)
3 pounds mutton or lamb, any cut can be used (rabbit and venison are also good)
1 to 2 onions, depending upon size and personal preference
9 cups water, more if needed as the stew simmers
4 to 5 medium-sized potatoes, peeled and quartered

Using pieces of inside pulp only, roast the green chilies after cutting them in half, removing the seeds, and pricking the skins in several places. Roast until both sides blister, then remove them from the oven and dunk them in cold water before peeling. This washes off some of the chili oil, which can burn sensitive skin, and makes them easier to peel.

Put meat and onions in a heavy pot and brown lightly, using the fat of the meat. Add remaining ingredients and bring stew to a boil. Reduce heat and simmer for 1½ to 2 hours or until meat and potatoes are soft. Add seasoning to taste after serving.

Note: Beans were the staple of the Indian diet even after the native menu was increased by the culinary contributions of the Spanish and Mexican cultures. This stew can be made without meat, using 2 to 3 cups of pinto, navy, or kidney beans and is very tasty with a combination of onions, chilies, and tomatoes.

Soak the beans overnight in enough water to cover them. Using this same water (and you may need to add more as the beans cook), bring the beans, onions, chilies, and tomatoes to a boil. Reduce the heat and simmer for about 3 hours or until the beans are soft but not mushy. If you find the chilies make the stew too hot, add a peeled and cut up raw potato. Be sure to remove the potato pieces before serving.

Tom Tochino was a Navajo. His Indian name is unrecorded. He is shown here in native garb, before he was sent to Christian missionary school where his hair was cut short and he was outfitted in Anglo attire.

Navajo warriors, following the custom of well-to-do Mexican men, often wore decorative pieces of gold and silver. His necklace is strung with a variety of crosses fashioned after those worn or used by the Spanish soldiers and priests.

Blankets such as Tochino is wearing are still made by the women of the Navajo nation (the largest American Indian tribe). The women raise sheep primarily for their wool which is dyed and woven into fine blankets both for bedding and wearing apparel. Photograph courtesy of Sharlot Hall Museum

Posole

Yield: about 6 servings

1 pound of lean pork shoulder or
    chops, cut into bite size pieces
2 14½-oz. cans yellow hominy
Juice of one lime
2 garlic cloves, crushed

1 cup chopped scallions
Dash oregano
1 teaspoon red chili powder
1 hominy can of water
1 cup chopped celery

Brown pork in skillet. Mix other ingredients in a large pot and after draining off fat, add pork. Bring to a slow boil; then simmer covered for about 1 hour.

Colonizers, in order to survive, must be good at adapting to the prevailing diet. When Coronado and his soldiers came north from Mexico in 1540, they relied heavily upon traditional Indian foods. Most of the recipes we know today as "Spanish" or "Mexican" are in effect a blending of Indian and Spanish. Many have been further adapted to family or regional change. Posole is a basic meat and corn combination which has many versions throughout the Southwest.

Chorizo Con Huevos
(Mexican Sausage with Eggs)

Eggs, of course are a universal food. Chorizo, the Mexican sausage, has a history similar to so many adaptive types of food. There was no sausage in Mexico or the Southwest before the Spanish came; however, various kinds of sausage were a tradition all throughout Europe.

Chorizo is a sausage adapted to what was available, and flavored to the Mexican palate. It is readily available in small markets and chain stores in the West. Chorizo Con Huevos makes a fine breakfast or brunch entree.

Yield: 1 serving

3 or 4 ounces chorizo
1 tablespoon oil
2 eggs

Cream or milk, as needed
Chopped scallions to taste
Avocado slices, for garnish

Remove skins from chorizos, crumble into a tablespoon of hot oil, and fry slowly. Beat eggs separately adding a little cream or milk and add to chorizo. Stir and fold as you would scrambled eggs. Before eggs set, add chopped scallions. Garnish with thin avocado slices and serve.

In March 1886 the five Babbitt brothers — David, Charles, George, William, and Edward — arrived in northern Arizona where they planned to settle and invest capital derived from the sale of all they had owned in Cincinnati, Ohio. Their combined talents were numerous and the ventures which they undertook included cattle and sheep raising and marketing; operating a network of trading posts on the Indian reservation; selling hardware, lumber, dry goods, foodstuffs, and clothing in Flagstaff, Winslow, Kingman, Holbrook, and Page as well as supplying smaller mercantile stores throughout both northern and southern Arizona; operating a mortuary, livery stable, and later representing several styles of the "horseless carriage." The Babbitt brothers also ran Flagstaff's first opera hall, ice house, and bank.

Like many other emigrants, they were interested in making a place for themselves in the new territory and almost one hundred years later, the contributions of the Babbitts are still being catalogued.

Gazpacho Salad

Yield: 8 servings

2 medium cucumbers, peeled and thinly sliced
2 teaspoons salt
⅔ cup olive oil
⅓ cup wine vinegar
1 garlic clove, minced
1 tablespoon chopped fresh basil or 1 teaspoon dried basil
½ teaspoon freshly ground pepper

10 medium mushrooms, sliced
4 scallions, cut up
½ teaspoon minced parsley
3 large tomatoes, peeled and cut into wedges
1 medium green pepper
½ pound Swiss cheese, thinly sliced
4 hard cooked eggs, sliced

Put cucumbers in a bowl. Sprinkle with 1 teaspoon salt and let stand for 30 minutes. In a large salad bowl combine oil, vinegar, garlic, basil, salt, and pepper. Add mushrooms and scallions. Drain cucumber slices, pat dry with paper towel, and add to ingredients in bowl. Top mixture with parsley and mix gently. Add a layer of tomatoes and green pepper. Cover the bowl and chill for 4 hours. Just before serving, add Swiss cheese and toss gently. Garnish with sliced eggs.

Chile Rellenos Casserole

4 ounces diced green chilies, drained
1 pound Monterey Jack cheese, grated
1 pound sharp Cheddar cheese

4 eggs, separated
⅔ cup evaporated milk
½ teaspoon salt
½ teaspoon pepper
1 tablespoon flour

Combine cheeses and chilies, and put in a greased casserole 12-by-8-by-2 inches. Beat egg whites until stiff. Blend egg yolks, milk, flour, salt and pepper. Add egg whites. Pour over cheese, using fork to ooze it through. Bake 60 minutes or until knife comes clean, in a 350 degrees F. oven. This can be prepared ahead and refrigerated before baking.

Chili Pie Con Queso

2 4-ounce cans green chilies
4 beaten eggs

¾ pound Monterey Jack cheese grated

Grease a pie plate. Line with chilies cut to lie flat. Cover with cheese, then eggs. Bake 1 hour at 300 degrees F. Serve hot, cut in wedges.

— Bruce Babbitt, Governor

Roasted Jojoba Nuts

Jojoba nuts are roasted at a low to moderate heat for about an hour and then ground.

Combine 1 heaping tablespoon of ground jojoba to each cup of water and stir. Boil approximately 4 minutes and strain into a cup. The crumbled shell of an egg will help the grounds settle faster. Lace to taste with milk or cream and sugar.

Jojoba has been a source of food for Indian gatherers over the centuries and also used medicinally. But it was of greatest interest to the mountain men and pioneers as a replacement for coffee. They called it the "coffee bush" because its seeds look just like coffee beans.

Walnuts and acorns are gathered in the Fall and enjoyed in a variety of ways. Yavapai Indians often used them in place of a missed meal. A delicious snack can be made by combining raw or roasted acorns, sunflower and pumpkin seeds, pinyon nuts, walnuts, and dried berries. Shelled nuts can be roasted at 300 degrees F. for 1 hour, stirring frequently so nuts brown evenly, and salted to taste. Also, ground nut meats may be mixed with wild honey for a delicious spread.

Drying and storing nuts, fruits, vegetables, and meat during the gathering season was important because only in this way could one prepare a meal or snack combining several different ingredients. This Apache Indian woman is preparing walnuts for winter use. Behind her (foreground) are bags of shelled corn. The walnut, like many other Indian foods, was often used in a variety of ways. The shells stained hands brown and did the same for graying hair and new cloth. The bark was considered to have medicinal properties, as well. Nogales (Arizona) is derived from nogal, the Spanish word for walnut. Photograph courtesy of the Department of Library, Archives and Public Records, State of Arizona

This photograph was taken in 1900 on the Apache hunting grounds of the Chiricahua Mountains in southeastern Cochise County. The meat these hunters are drying is bear, although "jerky" (so called because the Indians pulled or "jerked" strips of meat from the carcass) can be made from venison, elk, buffalo, lamb, or beef. Photograph courtesy of Sharlot Hall Museum

Gail Gardner's Jerky Recipe

Yield: 5 pounds raw meat will make 1 pound of jerky

Use a utility grade of beef (round steak is good) and trim it of all fat. Cut meat with the grain into strips about eight inches by two inches by one-eighth inch thick.

Bring a large pot of water to boil and salt it heavily, enough so that a raw potato will float. With a tong, slowly dip each piece of meat in the boiling brine. Place pieces on a wire rack to drain.

Pepper the moist strips with a coarse pepper, to taste. This will flavor as well as repel flies, and if any flies do contaminate it you will never know, thinking it is pepper. This will neither add to nor detract from the finished product.

Now comes the drying of the meat. On a solid wire strung like a clothes line, drape each strip over in an area protected from direct sunlight. Fat will turn rancid before the meat dries if in direct sunlight. A screen porch is ideal and early Fall is the best time of year. If the meat is not protected, the wild birds will eat it. Blue Jays are particularly fond of it. Let the strips dry for a week to ten days, depending on the climate.

When the jerky is stiff and solid, remove it from the wire and store in a clean sugar or flour sack, or any other suitable cloth bag. Hang the sack in the pantry or basement where light and moisture are minimal. Whatever you do, never tell one soul what you are making. Jerky bums outnumber politicians in cleverness and sheer numbers.

Jerky can be eaten as is. It is a nutritious snack, lacking only Vitamin C and animal fat. It's lightweight enough for backpackers and long distance runners, and loved by kids for hundreds of years. You can chop the strips up in a food processor, mix with flour and milk to make a gravy, and pour over hot biscuits, or add pieces to stew.

As early as the American Revolution, troops reported the use of jerky by Indian guides. Properly prepared, it will keep indefinitely, is easy to carry, and can be eaten as is or cooked in water to make a stew. Fur traders in the West made it, sometimes grinding the dried strips and adding equal parts of suet, dried nuts, and berries to make chunks of pemmican. The Mexican version of jerky, known as "carne seca," is seasoned with garlic and red chili powder in addition to salt and pepper.

Jerky
(Adapted)

   Trim all fat off round steak. Freeze the meat and when partially thawed, cut along the grain in long, thin strips. Pepper is not needed for the cosmetic purpose described previously but do season to taste with salt, pepper, garlic powder, chili powder, or onion powder. Place the meat strips on wire cake racks with foil underneath to catch any drippings. Place in a preheated oven at 150 to 200 degrees F. with the door open for escaping moisture. Turn meat several times over a period of six to eight hours; overnight is even better. After meat is *thoroughly* and evenly dried, store your jerky in a cloth bag or a jar with a tight-fitting lid. With either recipe for jerky preparation, complete secrecy is the key ingredient if you wish to enjoy any of the fruits of your labor.

A placer miner somewhere in the central mountains of Arizona, date unknown. Photograph courtesy of the Department of Library, Archives and Public Records, State of Arizona

John H. Marion was co-owner, along with Benjamin Weaver, of the *Arizona Miner*, Prescott's first newspaper and one of the most influential in the territory. He established the *Prescott Morning Courier* in 1881, served in a number of public offices, and was suggested for governor shortly before his death in 1891. But, like most of the others who came to the territory in its early days, John Marion started out as a crusty prospector. In an editorial in the *Arizona Miner* on September 16, 1873, he reminisced: "During the ten years that we have passed in Arizona, we have prospected, mined, risked our life among Indians, suffered hardships innumerable, sewed on many a button, flopped many a flap jack, and upon several occasions, gone to bed on Mother Earth, tired, hungry, and a little alarmed about the permanency of our scalp. During these long years, we were not strictly happy; no, indeed."

Frontier Living

The dishes which seem unique to the Southwest have actually evolved from the interaction of Indian, Spanish, Mexican, and Anglo lifestyles. Mountain men, pathfinders, soldiers, gold miners, cowboys, and pioneer families combined the best traditions of each culture and added their individual ethnic touches. The results were as varied and delightful as the colorful personalities who populated the Arizona Territory.

Regarding it as a hostile land — dry, difficult, and populated with Indians — few women elected to live on such a frontier. So men had no choice; they learned to cook, but the fare was basic to begin with. Young Kit Carson was cook for Ewing Young's expedition in 1829. Camped in Big Chino Valley on the headwaters of the Verde, Carson prepared deer, bear, and antelope dishes as well as trail provisions for the party. An incident in the life of the pioneer Indian scout, Wales Arnold, gives some insight into the simple but ample diet required for a rugged man.

He was one of General George Crook's most trusted scouts and lived most of his life in the wilds of the Arizona territory. Gail Gardner tells of Arnold returning to Fort Verde early one morning and entering a boarding house run by a retired soldier and his wife. His breakfast order was simple and explicit: "I want a can of peaches, six biscuits, a dozen eggs scrambled with a tin of green chilis, and a quart of hot coffee." It was done.

Frontiersmen lived by their wits and ate whatever was at hand simply because they learned to see the possibilities where others saw only a wilderness. Not only did oral traditions supplement the knowledge of each subsequent wave of settlers, but often physical resources — such as a blue speckled enamelware coffee pot or a well-seasoned Dutch oven — helped to make a canvas tent or log lean-to a little less dreary and a little more like the comfortable homes they had left behind.

A dutch oven (left foreground) is made of heavy cast iron and is from eight to sixteen inches around and several inches deep. A "spider" is a dutch oven with three stubby legs which can be placed securely directly on the coals of a campfire or hung from a hook above the fire by its handle. The lid fits tightly and has a rim to hold hot coals for complete cooking. Flat rocks can be placed inside to facilitate the proper browning of breads, cakes, and pies. In short, the dutch oven is the entire kitchen — kettle, frying pan, oven — all in one. While cooking with a dutch oven takes time, the savory results are worth waiting for. Photograph courtesy of Sharlot Hall Museum

"The American mining pioneer is a character that will bear examination. Physically no man is his equal. A dweller out of doors. A constant traveller, his exercise in the open air gives him a fine muscular development, great strength of wind and limb, a vigorous appetite, and a relish for the plainest food. What he would deem unpalatable in the East is here a pleasing meal. The toughest meat, coffee plain, beans and slap-jacks, these are better dishes to him than those prepared by the most expert French or Italian cooks. Nor is he particular about his table furniture, if indeed he has a table. A tin plate for his meat, a tin cup for his coffee, a tin pan for his beans, a hunting knife and a tin spoon compose his kit, and serve him acceptably. The earth is his bed, his saddle his pillow, and a blanket his covering, and he sleeps more soundly and sweetly than he would on the softest of couches. Removed from the marts of trade and freed from the restraints of society, with an eye to comfort and his business, rather than to fashion or show, he dresses with the utmost simplicity. When on Sundays and holidays he comes from the mountains to the towns out of respect to the occasion, and the remembrance of other days, he appears in a "boiled shirt" and polished boots, but he cannot disguise his discomfort, is ill at ease, and on the morrow returns to his old clothes with immense relief. To the pampered sons of luxury, the slaves of fashion in the East, the chequered life of the bronzed pioneer seems one of intolerable hardship and vicissitude, and yet what would they not give — the shattered victims of city life, the dyspeptic, the rheumatic, the neuralgic and gouty — for his keen appetite and robust health.''

an excerpt from The American Pioneer
An Oration
Delivered before the Arizona Pioneer Society,
at Prescott, July 4, 1866
By Governor Richard C. McCormick
Printed in the Arizona Miner *in July 1866*

Dutch Oven Roast

Yield: ½ pound of meat per person

Soap the outside of the oven to discourage soot build up, then preheat the oven and lid so heat won't be drawn out by the addition of cold ingredients. Into the oven drop a chunk of suet or fat trimmed from the beef cut you're about to cook. Coat the oven thoroughly with the fat, then brown the beef on all sides. Ease in a cup of hot water; *never* pour cold water into a hot oven because you run a good chance of cracking it. Always leave room at the top of the oven so the food doesn't touch the lid. About an hour before you want to serve, check the water level and add vegetables of your choice. As soon as you take the oven off the fire, remove the lid as moisture will build up on the under side and drip into your dinner. With proper attention, any of these dutch oven recipes can be prepared in your fireplace. Aspen and oak coals hold the heat the best and blacken pots and ovens the least.

"Burying" your dutch oven is a great way to slow cook a dish, and this method will tenderize the toughest game or oldest beans. Dig a hole in a sandy area completely free of humus and line the hole with rocks (or aluminum foil) to prevent heat loss. Cooking time varies from four to eight hours, but the only way you can overcook a dish is if the water totally evaporates. Cooking time can be shortened by building another fire on top of the buried dutch oven. If you don't do this, it's a good idea to place several easily identifiable rocks as a marker on top of the spot.

Most important, *never* soak or scour your dutch oven as it will rust, and *never* blame anyone but yourself if you can't remember where you buried dinner.

Dutch Oven Apples

Wash and core six to eight large apples, being careful not to pierce the bottoms. Fill centers with a mixture of brown sugar, raisins, butter, cinnamon, and cook's choice of spices. Place the filled apples on a greased pie tin holding a small amount of water, not more than one cupful. Put the pie tin in the oven on top of pebbles or flat rocks. Cover with lid and bake thirty minutes buried. If you don't want to bury the oven, cook it on a bed of red hot coals and place coals on the lid with a shovel. The rim will hold them in place. Cook for about 20 minutes, but check the amount of water and the doneness of the apples from time to time. You may need to add or replace coals to speed the cooking or add ashes to the coals to cool down the baking temperature.

Usually dried fruit was the only kind available on the trail or in remote settlements. Canned fruits were too heavy to pack in wagons or on mules, and fresh fruit was bruised past recognition by the bouncing it took over the rough terrain. "Fresh" apples and peaches which had traveled overland from California or St. Louis for several months brought $1.00 each in Prescott.

Blueberry Spider Cake

4 cups flour
1 teaspoon salt
4 level teaspoons baking powder
½ cup (1 stick) butter

1 quart blueberries
Milk as needed
1 tablespoon butter

Sift together flour, salt, and baking powder. Rub the flour into ½ cup butter. Wash and drain the blueberries and dredge with flour. Add the berries to the flour and butter mixture; mix well and add just enough milk to make a dough soft enough to spread in the pan, but not run. Heat 1 tablespoon butter in a spider and spread the dough in it about ¾ inches thick. Set it over a moderate fire to cook slowly about 20 minutes, allowing 10 minutes for each side. Shake the spider from time to time and turn the cake to prevent burning. When done, split the cake open, butter thickly, and serve at once.

Cooked and Poached Eggs

Anything can be spoiled in the cooking and nothing more easily than eggs. As a matter of fact, eggs should never be boiled. When eggs are to be served in the shell, they should first be well covered with boiling water and then placed where the water will keep near the boiling point for five or six minutes. Poached eggs should be dropped in boiling water, well salted, covered closely and set back to cook slowly. To cream eggs, grease a hot spider with butter, put in a half cup of cream (farmer's cream), break in the eggs, cover closely, and cook very slowly to avoid tough, leathery eggs.

The first use of the word "cow boy" described outlaw marauders who were loyal to the English crown during the American Revolution. They particularly infested the neutral ground near New York City and were so called because they rang cow bells to lure colonial farmers into the bush in search of stray animals.

In 1836 Ewing Young led one of the early western cattle drives, herding Mexican stock northward from California. But it wasn't until after the Civil War that the term "cowboy" was used in its present meaning. The Spanish vaquero, from "vaca" meaning cow, supplied most of the equipment, terms, and flavor of the American cowboy.

Charles Hollingshead (shown left with two unidentified cowboys) was a man typical of that independent and colorful breed of men. Born in Utah on June 29, 1864, he evidenced a mastery of animals at a very early age and began breaking horses when he was only eight years old. He came to Arizona in May of 1887, arriving in Flagstaff on the 17th, and immediately began to earn a reputation as a top "broncbuster." Charles, at twenty-three, was known to be exceptionally strong, "and so the slogan" he wrote in his journal, "'don't give Hollingshead your rope to put on a horse that will try to get away.'"

In the early 1890s "Buffalo Bill" Cody saw him in Flagstaff where Charles had taken horses to sell. Cody was greatly impressed with his skills and asked Hollingshead to join his wild west show and tour the world. He agreed and attended the World's Columbia Exposition at Chicago in 1893. Charles Hollingshead held top honors in world champion riding, roping, and broncbusting. It was an exciting experience, but soon he tired of the limelight and returned to ranching in Campe Verde.

Another man who traveled with Buffalo Bill's wild west show was "Arizona Charlie" Meadows, one of the participants in the first organized rodeo where admission was charged and prizes awarded which was held in Prescott on July 4, 1888. After traveling to Africa, Australia, and China in the late 1880s, Arizona Charlie landed in San Francisco where he sold a promoter named Clark on the feasibility of a wild west show headed by himself. Meadows talked Clark into coming to Phoenix where there were cowboys from all over the territory and a whole reservation full of Indians to choose from. Meadows selected the finest cowboys available, including Stewart Knight of Chino Valley and Charles Hollingshead of Campe Verde, whose job it was to break the stock used in the show. After a long run in Arizona and parts of California, Arizona Charlie's Wild West Show played to Prescott audiences on July 3 and 4, 1897.

Just a few months before their appearance, on May 9, another animal trained by Hollingshead was used in a jail break get-away. Charles wrote in his journal: "I broke gray Frank the [Sheriff George] Ruffner H̄ saddle horse that Jim Parker rode away after killing [Deputy District Attorney] Ross of Prescott, after ordering horse saddled at the Barn at the Point of Death." "Sure Shot" was Sheriff Ruffner's favorite mount and was permanently crippled during Parker's attempt to elude trackers.

Charles Hollingshead left very exact instructions in his journal on how to "brake a horse gentle":

> "Rope a wild horse by front feet throw him down. Hog tie him, put rope on his neck, and on his nose, then let him up when he runs, double him up show him he cant get away — that helps to learn him to stand tied. tie him to solid post, let him learn by himself to stand tied long enough to want some relief — give him little feed, some water, when he nickers at you, then he is said to be learned your tricks — then gentle his nose for that is what he sences everything with, then gentle his head by rubing him all over head then gentle his neck by learning him to lead, that way wises him so you can be director instead of the horse, then handle his legs until gentle. then brake the body by riding, he is in a negative frame of mind, then teach him the things you want him to know. a horse hardly ever learns more than the teacher, always be kind but firm   The man who has trouble with his horse in the man who does not know enough to teach the horse. Horses are very brainey   the next to woman for Intelligence."

In 1902 to 1903 Charles Hollingshead (shown here circa 1910) worked as an officer on the Mexican Border Patrol. Although he was an expert marksman, it went against his grain to shoot at people. He chose instead to quit policing the border, and returned once again to Camp Verde. There he began writing stories of his true adventures in the Arizona Territory. He enjoyed reading and did so by lamplight for many winter hours. He studied the teachings of a school of Mental Science and obtained a degree as a Doctor of Mental Science on February 26, 1912. But, first and foremost he was a cowboy.

On November 6, 1937 Charles Hollingshead died. It was said of him that during his lifetime he could gentle any horse, lift a wagon off the ground, and was a crack shot. Whatever he attempted, he put his soul into and never feared God, man, or devil.

You couldn't ask more from a man. Photographs courtesy of Sharlot Hall Museum

Cowboy Coffee

Place about 1 tablespoon of coffee per cup of water or a handful of coffee for a gallon pot of water in a flour or sugar sack, cotton sock, or levi leg and tie firmly. Add to the boiling water and remove from fire when brew is strong enough (about 3 to 5 minutes). Slowly add about ½ cup cold water to settle grounds. Serve straight or lace with cream and sugar.

Cornmeal Coffee

This was originally made in a dutch oven when the Arbuckle coffee ran out on the trail or in remote camps and settlements. Canned milk was usually used because it was easier to obtain and store and its quality more predictable.

2 cups Indian cornmeal — blue or white
½ cup sugar

1 teaspoon cinnamon
1 cup hot milk per person

Brown cornmeal in a pan, stirring often so it doesn't scorch. Remove from heat and add the sugar and cinnamon. Using about 2 heaping tablespoons per cup, stir it into hot milk.

In the early days, cowboys often packed their supplies on mules or horses and ran a "greasy sack outfit," which meant that they did their own cooking. But, as conditions on the range improved, the demands of the cowboy increased until some of the better wranglers wouldn't sign on for cattle drives or roundup if the "credentials" of the camp cook weren't up to snuff.

The importance of the cook was so great that he was second in command and took orders only from the trail boss, if he asked nicely. The cook not only served meals but he also tended the cowboys' bedrolls; cleaned their clothes; treated their wounds; kept the camp, the cook fire, and all supplies (including the tobacco ration) in order; cut hair; and was arbitrator of any differences of opinion. His word was final and it was not smart to rile the cook.

A chuck wagon, like the one shown here, was often just an ordinary conveyance outfitted for the trail — but it was the cook's exclusive domain. It contained shelves for storage and the lid folded down to serve as a preparation area and dining table. While cowboys ate an often monotonous fare of beans, beef, biscuits, bacon, and coffee there were variations based on availability and degree of desperation. A favorite during Spring and Fall roundup were Lamb Fries and Rocky Mountain Oysters (sheep and calf testicles) which could be cooked in hot water over the fire, or roasted in the ashes until they popped, or fried in fat until crisp. Rattlesnake meat was fancied by some who swore it tasted just like breast of chicken.

These unidentified men enjoyed a less exotic meal somewhere in the central mountains of Arizona around the turn of the century. Photograph courtesy of Sharlot Hall Museum

Manloff Benson came to the Arizona territory in January or February 1875 and because of his Civil War experience with the 3rd Iowa Infantry, was hired as an Indian scout at Fort Whipple. Although he was only in the area for a short time, Prescott must have made a lasting impression on him. His son, Prescott Arizona Benson, worked in the mines around Globe in the early part of the century and descendants still reside in Arizona. —Information contributed by
Prescott "Scott" Benson
Phoenix, Arizona

The Army provided a number of the early surveyors of the area now known as Arizona and protected emigrants as best they could considering the territorial military officials were headquartered in the security of Santa Fe, New Mexico, almost 500 miles east. But when Governor Goodwin and his party insisted on heading into the central mountains, it was decided that a fortress should be provided to protect them and the settlers who would inevitably flock to the newly-established territorial capital. Fort Whipple, shown here in an 1864 drawing, was named for Lieutenant Amiel W. Whipple, one of the Army surveyors who traversed this area in 1853 to 1854. While Fort Yuma was a far better known post, — soldiers and civilians alike joked that a trooper who died and went to Hades sent back word to his friends at Fort Yuma to forward his blankets — Fort Whipple was considered the most superior assignment in the territory and one reserved as a reward for those who distinguished themselves in skirmishes with the Indians or in the salons of Washington. In 1870 Whipple Barracks became headquarters for the Military Department of Arizona, with General George Crook as commander. In May of 1885 one company of colored troops, Company "B" of the Tenth Cavalry, were also stationed at Fort Whipple.

Today, Whipple no longer serves as a post for Indian fighters and "Buffalo Soldiers" but is instead one of the finest Veterans Administration hospitals in the nation. Photograph courtesy of the Department of Library, Archives and Public Records, State of Arizona

While Fort Whipple was considered "easy duty" with dress parades, band concerts, receptions for military and civilian dignitaries, social calls back and forth between the post and the capital, and only an occasional distracting "unpleasantness," other Army officers and enlisted men were not so lucky. Troopers earned thirteen dollars a month which they wasted on over-priced "benzine" whiskey, rigged gambling tables, and disease-ridden prostitutes during infrequent breaks in the boredom. Most of the time out of camp was spent following cold trails of Indians who were masters at hit and run tactics which the soldiers were untrained and poorly equipped to match. Duty in the southern half of Arizona was made even more unbearable by putrid water, dust storms, tainted rations, and heavy uniforms.

    The wives of Army officers were considered as necessary evils and officially ignored, being catagorized as "camp followers." They learned to rise above the indignities of Army regulations and life, attempting to retain a semblance of civilization. It was this feeling, and the regimental camaraderie shared by the soldiers, that inspired such photographs as this one taken at the Army post on the San Carlos Indian reservation in the 1880s. Troops abandoned the post soon after Geronimo and his clan were shipped by train to a reservation in Florida. The flowers withered, the buildings crumbled in upon themselves, and the site is now underwater. Photograph courtesy of the Department of Library, Archives and Public Records, State of Arizona

Food was not needed merely to sustain life. For the women living on remote Army posts, the preparation and enjoyment of a meal was a link with civilization and their past lives "back in the States."

Potatoes were usually plentiful and sold for about five cents a pound, and so this was often the main ingredient for a variety of recipes from main dishes to dainty candies. On the other hand, eggs were two dollars a dozen and seldom available. While the cost of a pound of butter began at two dollars, it was worth its weight in gold. Some suppliers charged double these prices if the customer paid in greenbacks, or "Lincoln skins" as they were derisively called. While mock maple syrup and soup for breakfast might remind one of home, the cowboy and the miner often longed for delicacies such as oysters, as did the lieutenant's lady from Nantucket.

Mock Maple Syrup

Yield: about 1½ cups

2 cups brown sugar
1 cup sugar
1 cup water

Pinch cream of tartar
1 teaspoon good vanilla extract

Add brown sugar, granulated sugar, and cream of tartar to water. Boil 5 minutes. When cool add vanilla.

Baked Beans

Yield: 8 to 10 servings

1 quart navy beans
2 tablespoons sugar
1 pound half lean and fat meat

or ½ pound of all fat pork
Salt to taste
Pepper to taste

Soak navy beans in water overnight. In morning drain off the water, and pour on boiling water. Let the beans parboil, and when the skins begin to crack, add sugar, meat, salt and pepper to taste, and bake all the afternoon. Nice for Saturday night supper.

Baked Bean Soup

Yield: depends on how much is left over from Saturday

Left over beans
1 onion
3 or 4 whole cloves

Salt and pepper to taste
3 hard-cooked eggs, sliced
1 lemon, sliced

Take the cold beans left from Saturday's baking, and put them in a stewpan with onion, and cloves. Cover them with cold water, and boil till soft; then press them through a strainer and return to stove; season with salt and pepper to taste. Add sliced eggs and lemon, when sending to the table. If one prefers a thinner soup, omit lemon and eggs.

Chicken Soup

Yield: 6 to 8 servings

1 chicken
1 sprig parsley, minced
1 stalk celery, minced
1 small onion, minced

Cream, as needed
1 tablespoon flour
1 tablespoon butter

Cut up chicken and cover with cold water. Add parsley, celery, and onion. Boil until meat drops from the bones; then remove chicken and strain broth. Stand liquor in a cool place and when fat forms hard on top, remove it in a cake. Measure broth and for each pint allow a pint of cream. Heat broth to a boil in one saucepan and the cream in another. Rub flour and butter smoothly together and stir into boiling broth. Let boil, stirring constantly for 2 or 3 minutes, then gradually stir in the scaled cream. Cook about a minute, and serve at once.

Potato and Oyster Soup

Yield: 8 to 10 servings

6 potatoes, chopped fine
4 onions, chopped fine
2 quarts milk
Butter the size of an egg

Salt to taste
Pepper to taste
1 or 2 pints oysters

Boil potatoes and onions in water enough to cover. When potatoes are soft, mash through a colander or sieve and return to the kettle. Scald milk. Add milk, butter, salt, and pepper to taste. Bring to a boil; then add oysters, boil 1 minute, and serve at once.

Oyster Fritters

Yield: 8 to 10 medium sized fritters

1 pint oysters
Butter to taste
1 or more tablespoons flour
1 egg yolk

Juice of ½ lemon
Salt to taste
1 beaten egg
Cracker crumbs

Heat the oysters in their own liquor, then drain and chop them fine. Season with butter, and add a little oyster liquor thickened with flour. Add the juice of lemon and salt to taste. Mix well and when cold shape into little fritters, dip in beaten egg, roll in cracker crumbs, and fry in deep, hot fat until golden brown.

Tomato Escalop

This dish has the advantage of presenting in attractive and tasty form the substantials of a satisfactory meal, while at the same time each ingredient therein may be a leftover, and the most "finicky" member of the household none the wiser.

Yield: depends on how many leftovers are used

Into a greased baking dish slice a layer of cold boiled potatoes, and over this strew cold cooked meat which has been put through a meat grinder. Over this, layer tomatoes, either fresh or canned, seasoning all with butter, pepper, and salt. Continue the triple layers until the dish is full, being sure that there is enough juice in the tomatoes to moisten all. Bake slowly, and long enough to blend the flavors (325 degrees F. for about 45 minutes). Those who like tomatoes at all will relish them in this way, and it is a good method of using up cold meat which would otherwise be difficult to manage, such as cold steaks and bits of sausage.

Tomato Conserves

Yield: 6 large canning jars

9 pounds tomatoes	ground cloves and cinnamon
3 pounds (6 cups) sugar	1 quart vinegar
2 ounces (4 tablespoons)	

Add tomatoes, sugar, ground cloves, and cinnamon to vinegar. Simmer for four hours. When cool, seal in sterilized jars.

Potato Candy

There is only one way to cook potatoes: that is, to steam them, which will cook them much quicker and make them dry, rich, and tasteful without burning. One of them will nourish you as much as two prepared in any other way.

Yield: 1 dozen

1 small potato	or bottled cherries
Butter to taste	1 teaspoon vanilla extract
1 cup nuts, chopped	Confectioners' sugar, as needed
1 cup or less candied cherries	

Boil potato until it is soft. Drain and mash with a bit of butter. Add chopped nuts, cherries, and vanilla. Take it on the molding board and add confectioners' sugar, kneading until it will take no more sugar. Flatten out, cut in squares, and lay on waxed paper to cool.

Mashed Potato Candy

Yield: About 3 dozen

¾ cup warm mashed potatoes, seasoned with 2 tablespoons of butter, if desired
4 cups confectioners' sugar
4 cups shredded coconut
1½ teaspoons vanilla extract

½ teaspoon salt
One 8-ounce bar of melted German sweet chocolate *or* a small package of semi-sweet chocolate pieces

Mix together potatoes and sugar, then add all other ingredients except the chocolate. Blend well; the mixture will be stiff. Press into a buttered pan large enough that the candy will be about ½ inch thick. Pour the melted chocolate over the top, spreading evenly. Chill. Cut in squares.

There were any number of ingredients which were not available to army wives on remote posts a century ago. Viola Koenig, Home Economist for the Yavapai County Extension Office of the University of Arizona, contributed a modern version of this old favorite.

Dried Apple Cake

Yield: 2 loaves

3 cups dried apples
3 cups molasses
1 cup seedless raisins
3 cups flour
1 cup (2 sticks) butter
3 eggs

1 teaspoon baking soda
1 teaspoon salt
1 teaspoon ground cloves
1 teaspoon cinnamon
1 teaspoon allspice
1 teaspoon nutmeg

Soak dried apples overnight in water to cover. Chop and mix them with molasses. Stew until almost soft. Add raisins and stew a little longer. Cool and add flour, butter, eggs, salt, cloves, cinnamon, allspice, and nutmeg.

Note: No further instructions are available, but the authors suggest baking batter in two greased loaf pans at 350 degrees F. for 30 minutes or until cake tests done.

Spice Cake

1 heaping tablespoon butter
½ cup sugar
½ cup of molasses
1 egg, well-beaten
½ cup sweet milk
½ teaspoon cinnamon

½ teaspoon nutmeg
¼ teaspoon ground cloves
Flour, as needed
1 teaspoon baking powder
⅔ cup seeded and chopped
   raisins

To butter, sugar, molasses, egg, sweet milk, cinnamon, nutmeg, and cloves add enough flour to make quite stiff. Sift the baking powder in with the flour. Coat raisins with flour and add last. Bake in a shallow bread pan in a slow oven (325 degrees F. for 1 hour or until cake tests done). This cake will keep for several weeks if rolled in a cloth and placed in a tin cake box.

One-Half Pudding

Yield: 4 servings

½ cup sugar
½ cup (1 stick) butter
½ cup sour milk
½ cup chopped raisins
½ cup molasses
2 cups flour

1 teaspoon soda
½ teaspoon cinnamon
½ teaspoon nutmeg
½ teaspoon ground cloves
½ teaspoon salt

Combine above ingredients. Steam 1½ hours. Serve with vanilla sauce.

Vanilla Sauce
2 teaspoons cornstarch
2 cups sugar
1 cup (2 sticks) butter, melted
4 eggs, beaten

¼ teaspoon salt
10 tablespoons condensed milk
2 to 3 teaspoons vanilla extract

Cook all ingredients except vanilla in a double boiler, stirring continuously until thick. Add vanilla. Serve over Pudding.

Journey Cake

Journey Cakes were so called because they were cooked for the journey west and eaten when a fire could not be made. They were also prepared on the trail and sometimes used in place of a missed meal when emigrants had to hurry along.

2 cups yellow cornmeal	2 cups buttermilk
½ cup flour	2 tablespoons molasses
1 teaspoon baking soda	2 eggs, beaten
1 teaspoon salt	2 tablespoons butter, melted

Mix cornmeal with flour, baking soda, and salt. Stir in buttermilk, molasses, eggs, and butter. Pour into a greased 9-inch pan and bake at 425 degrees F. for 25 minutes.

This wagon train is crossing the Gila River near San Carlos in 1880. The wagons were called "movers outfits" because they moved a family and all their worldly possessions to their new home. Sharlot Mabridth Hall who came to Prescott two years later at the age of twelve wrote: "Perhaps a milk cow would be tied behind and a slat coop fastened to the rear end of the wagon would hold a few chickens; for there were neither chickens nor cattle nor any domestic animals to be had except as the settlers brought them. Always there were children peeping out under the wagon cover or trotting behind in the dusty road.

"It was often months between opportunities to renew the supply of food and clothing and every 'mover wagon' carried as much food as possible. Flour, bacon and coffee, enough to last six months was the rule and clothing for the whole family for a year was stored away under the high wagon bows. Sometimes room was found for a few bits of furniture, or a cook stove — a luxury in a place where a big open fireplace, a Dutch oven, a long-handled frying pan and a few iron pots constituted a well-furnished kitchen, and rough home-made furniture was the only kind to be had.

"The women and children gathered wood and built the camp fires and prepared supper, and as night closed in the children played among the wagons while the women sat by the fires talking, cooking the next day's food, or mending the travel-worn clothing. At this distance, we see only the romance but it was no easy experience. Days, weeks, months of slow journeying toward a strange land to make a home among unknown conditions, far from friends and relatives; the jolting, noisy wagons; the exposure to all weather; the scant means for comfort or cleanliness; the scant help in time of sickness — it was no romance but stern reality to the brave women who lived it day by day." Photograph courtesy of the Department of Library, Archives and Public Records, State of Arizona

Beaten Biscuits

The leavening for these biscuits is provided by the air which is beaten into the dough, so the "lightness" of the finished product depends on the strength and durability of the cook's arm.

Yield: 3 to 4 dozen

1 quart (4 cups) flour   1 cup thin cream

Knead thoroughly until soft and pliable, then pound with a wooden mallet or the flat side of an axe for half an hour. When the dough reaches the stage that a little piece pulls off with a snappy sound, mold it into small biscuits, making an indentation in the center with the thumb. Prick with a fork, place on greased tins and bake in a moderately hot oven (375 degrees F. for 10 minutes or until browned).

Sourdough Starter

Water that potatoes had been boiled in was often used to encourage the fermentation process.

Put approximately 3 parts of flour, 2 parts lukewarm water, and 1 part sugar together and let it stand covered on the back of the stove or somewhere where it will remain at a warm, constant temperature (80 to 90 degrees F.) but will *not* cook.

If your starter is sticky and strongly resembles glue, you're on the right track! Overnight the mixture will begin to ferment and you will see the mix bubbling and smell a yeast odor. Avoid mixing the starter too much as this lessens the gases needed to raise the dough. As you use the sourdough, add more flour, sugar, and water to replenish your starter.

Remember, if your mixture varies in temperature too drastically or if it goes too long without being renewed (two weeks or more), it can't be used. A scalded earthen crock or large glass jar is a good container to keep it in; never keep starter in a metal container. When cold weather sets in, wrap a blanket around your crock. If a freeze is forecasted, curl up around the crock under your bed covers.

The pioneer housewife had no baker or brewer to depend on for her yeast — she brought it with her by frequent renewals on the road or learned to make "sourdough" bread and biscuits that were the staff of life on the old trails. She could bake a loaf in an iron pot in a bed of coals if a stove or Dutch oven was lacking, or failing the pot, could cook thin biscuits in the frying pan.

Sourdough Starter
(Adapted)

1 cake yeast
2 cups lukewarm water, divided
2½ cups flour

Soak yeast in 1 cup lukewarm water for ½ hour. Add 1 cup lukewarm water and flour. Place in a crock and keep in a warm place. In about 12 hours it should be bubbly and ready to use. Take from the crock only what you will need in a recipe and never return leftover sourdough to container. Replenish the starter after each use with 2 parts flour to 1 part water.

Many camp cooks made thin biscuits by putting the sourdough starter in the top of a flour sack and mixing it there. Unless you're an expert at this technique, a bowl is easier to manage.

Sourdough Biscuits
Yield: 3 dozen biscuits

About 1 cup sourdough starter
Pinch salt
½ teaspoon baking soda
Flour, as needed

Sugar to taste
2 teaspoons baking powder
 (not double-acting)

Pinch off starter and put in center of flour in a bowl. Sprinkle salt and soda mixed with a little flour. Add sugar to taste and baking powder. Knead all ingredients into starter just until stickiness is gone. Roll out to about ¾-inch thickness and cut out biscuits. Place in lightly greased pans and let stand 45 minutes or until biscuits have doubled in size. Bake in a quick oven, about 400 to 425 degrees F. until golden brown.

Note: A Sourdough loaf can be made in the same way. Brush top with butter and slash. Bake at 400 degrees F. for 15 minutes, then reduce heat and continue baking until a golden brown.

Elderberry Pie

Elderberries
1 cup sugar

1 tablespoon good vinegar
Milk to taste

Line a pie tin with rich paste (pastry), fill with fresh elderberries, sprinkle with sugar and vinegar, cover with a top crust, wash it over with a little milk, and bake in a good oven (325 degrees F. for 1 hour or until crust is golden).

George Washington Barnard arrived at the Walker Diggings sometime in 1863. Perhaps the pickin's weren't as profitable as he'd hoped because by 1864 he had opened the first restaurant in Prescott, dubbed the Juniper House because it was near a large tree of that species. He had no stove, but did the cooking over a campfire and served up the best the country afforded — coffee, bread, and fried venison. Stewed dried apples served as dessert and slapjacks with sugar syrup, called "lick," were served for breakfast. The cost per meal was one dollar in gold, or two dollars in paper.

A. F. Banta remembered: "Dan White and I, both bullwhackers for Charley Beach, had played 'bean poker' all night in a wagon box, and being Sunday morning we went up early to the juniper tree and ate the first two meals put up by that prince of caterers, George W. Barnard."

When the Ehle and Osborn families arrived, they brought with them several milch cows and occasionally Barnard would have a pint or two of milk on hand. George would then display a large sign stating that there was "Milk For Coffee Today." By July 4, 1864 his fare had increased considerably according to the *Arizona Miner*: breakfast till 9 A.M. — beefsteak, venison steak, biscuits, hot cakes, fried liver, mutton chops, tea, coffee, and milk. Dinner, 12 to 3-mutton broth, beef potpie, venison potpie, mutton potpie, bean soup, beef soup, one quarter of a beef barbequed, two deer barbequed, sixty-four sheep barbequed, and apple roll with sauce. He also had purchased sixty-two pounds of elderberries (at $1.00 a pound) for pies and used some of these to pay Sam Miller for hauling pine logs to build tables and a spacious twelve-by-fifteen-foot dining hall roofed with several wagon covers.

With the discovery of gold in Granite Creek, the area began attracting miners and settlers. Arriving at their destination after weary weeks on the trail, there was little improvement in the situation. Although gold was abundant, there was considerable grumbling over the lack of goods and services to spend it on. Merely finding sufficient food and preparing it for use was no small thing in a land so lately wilderness and so far from any source of supplies. Every article used in the new community came from California and first was packed over the mountains from Wickenburg on mules. When Margaret Ehle and her husband Joseph arrived in mid-1864, flour was forty-four dollars a sack in greenbacks and bacon seventy-five cents a pound in gold dust. Flour was so scarce that often the supply on hand had to be divided and a few pounds given to each family.

Women like Margaret Ehle (shown here on her eighty-fifth birthday, October 14, 1902) had few illusions about life in the Arizona territory. They were self-reliant and were prepared for hardships, Indians, disease, and death. "Grandmother" Ehle had lived on the westward-moving frontier all her life and was one of Prescott's most valuable resources in its early days. She participated in all aspects of community life from the birthing of babies to last rites over lonely gravesites. Photograph courtesy of Sharlot Hall Museum

Lois and Ed Bobblett came with a wagon train from Colorado in the second week of July, 1864. The last leg of the journey from Albuquerque, New Mexico was particularly dangerous but Lois writes:

"We finally got through and in town [Prescott] there were only a few small boarding houses. We set up our camp and in the morning a one-eyed man came to our camp. His name was Holiday and said, 'Say, there are nine of us that want a place to board. Can't you board us?' Ed said, 'Why, there is a hotel here. Can't you board there?' 'Yes,' he said, 'But we are members of the legislature and we are from the north and the southern delegates are all there and a fight is on for the capital, and we want to board where we can talk things over by ourselves.' Ed told them we could board them if we could get anything to cook. 'Oh,' he said, 'There is plenty here to cook and we can eat off tin plates under a pine tree.' We went to work and set our wagon boxes down on the ground and put a ridge pole up between them, sewed the wagon sheets together and then put the wagon boxes just as far apart as we could and had the sheets up high enough to turn the rain. Then we sewed sheets in the gable ends and that made a dining room. We fixed a place outside to cook and the next day we started a boarding house in a tent under a big pine tree with nine of the first legislators that ever met in Arizona. Of course this was in the time of the rebellion. We were close to the hotel and the people that kept it were Seceders. We found out that the Southerners were intending to come in and massacre all the Northerners in the place, but one of their outfit got drunk and told it. Then all the Northerners got together and armed themselves and they stood guard every night for a long time."

After this incident, the Bobletts moved "out on the Mohave road, about fifty miles from Prescott," where they settled.

"We had to camp out till we got our cabin built. We had to get poles as there were nothing else near enough that we dared to go after so they cut poles about six inches through and built our house and put poles on top, then a lot of brush, next a lot of grass and covered all with about a foot of dirt. We made port holes, two on each side of the house so we could peek out to look for Indians. Of course we always kept them stopped up only when we thought there might be Indians around, especially after night. Many a time we were up nearly all night watching for Indians. We never lit a light so they could not see us and we could always tell by the way the dogs acted and barked whether they were barking at Indians or some wild animal. We entertained Governor McCormick, the first governor, in this pole house with dirt roof and dirt floor. We often entertained the government officers and their wives.

"One time I well remember, we were out of provisions. We knew a train loaded with government supplies was due but just when it would get in, we could not tell, so we had to pinch ourselves pretty hard to get along till it came in. Before it came we had eaten the last thing we had which was a little rice boiled with a little salt for our breakfast. About one o'clock the teams came in sight.

53

We had plenty of money to buy with but when they got there, (this was in the fall and it was raining, sleeting, and bitterly cold) there was a large family with two teams loaded, one was loaded with provisions to sell in Prescott, so Ed came in and said, 'Lois, we can get anything we want now,' and told me there was a woman and a lot of little children alone, so I went out and asked them in out of the storm. After they had gotten warm I said to the lady, I think their names were Hart, 'If I had anything to cook I would ask you all to stay and I would get you a warm supper but we ate the last we had for breakfast.' 'Oh, no,' she said, 'We have plenty in our wagons, we only wanted to get warm.' Well, they got warm and went back to their wagons. Ed wanted to buy some provisions from the men but, no, he was afraid Ed was not offering as much as it was worth in town and he would not let us have an ounce of anything. Ed told him just what the prices were the last time we got our supplies and offered, if they had raised, to make the difference good but he would not sell. Ed told me when he came to the house, he would try the wagon master and see what he could do and if he could not get anything from him, he would take his rifle and go out to the man and tell him to dig up something for us to eat or he would shoot him down. I begged him not to do that for we would not starve till we could get to town but the wagon boss let us have a sack of cornmeal and some bacon and sugar and coffee so we were all right for a time.

"Several of the men with Ed Boblett and myself took two yoke of cattle and went up to Prescott, a distance of about fifty miles, after provisions, but before the men went up to what we named Grief Hill, they found they could get an easier road up a ravine. We brushed it out and went up the ravine. It was a long hard pull for the oxen even with the empty wagons, so all walked. I never saw such a variety of flowers anywhere in my life, also some beautiful flowering shrubs I had never seen before or since. When we reached the top of the divide we all got in and rode till we came to a creek and here we had to camp all night. There had been a hail storm and we shoveled nearly a foot deep of hailstones off the ground to make our beds on the ground. This must have been in the latter part of May. In the morning we started and got through and put up at the hotel that we camped near when we boarded the nine men of the legislature. Here we found the two children that I spoke of before, that their mother had said to me she would give them away if she could find someone that would take them that had no children. I asked how these children came to be here and Mrs. Osburn (sic), the land lady, told me that their mother had died and they had the children. When they got supper for the family we sat down with them to eat. There was plenty of room for all but these two poor orphans had to wait till we were done, then they could eat what was left. It hurt me terribly to see that.

"We stayed at Prescott for a day or two with another family by the name of Aile [Ehle]. They had a large family of their own. I told Mrs. Aile what I saw and she said we ought to take them, but we thought maybe the Indians were so bad we might lose everything and have to walk out, or maybe get killed, and we did not want any children there to worry over. As soon as we moved back there, these officers came to us and told us they had taken the children from these people. It seemed they had promised their mother they would never separate them but one of their own girls got married and they gave the little girl, two-and-a-half years old, to her for a servant girl, and she made her wash all the dishes. One day they had meat for dinner and the poor little girl went to wash the platter and it was so heavy she let it fall, and the dish broke to pieces. The woman whipped her till she carried the marks for two weeks and the officers took them both and took them to the Ailes and hired them to take care of them till they could find someone to take them. They came to us and asked us to take them so we did. Flour was $50.00 a barrel and bacon 75 cents a pound; sugar, coffee, tea and any kind of dried fruit were all 75 cents a pound. Butter was $2.00 a pound, eggs $2.00 a dozen. Common calico 50 cents a yard. Any kind of cheap dress goods $1.50 a yard, so it was quite an undertaking but many a sack of flour and many a dress for the little girl was given us by the soldiers. One day a soldier took Charley, the boy, to the store and gave him a suit of clothes from hat to shoes and socks. That helped us out wonderfully. Charley was four years old and Isabel Jane was two-and-a-half years old when we took them. Their surname was Kerr and came from Missouri. We never knew whether they had any relatives or not."

In 1873 Alfred B. Spence, his wife Matilda, and his father-in-law, R. J. Lambuth, arrived from Missouri and settled on Groom Creek where they operated a sawmill. In 1875 they moved to Crook Canyon and constructed this log house. The location was selected because it was halfway between Prescott and the Peck Mine, which was then one of the most prosperous mines in the territory.

The original log structure was built in the manner typical of pioneer cabins and had two downstairs rooms and a large sleeping loft upstairs. In 1890 when lumber was more readily available, the board and batten kitchen was added. Here at Palace Station many a meal was prepared for weary travelers on the Prescott to Phoenix stage, and the horses were also watered and rested. Wagon freighters, miners, and mule skinners with pack trains carrying ore or supplies comprised the majority of overnight guests. For fifty cents one could buy a meal, one dollar purchased a space in the sleeping loft, and hay or grain for the livestock was provided at one dollar fifty cents a head.

The Spences raised six daughters, two sons, and two grandchildren here. Shown in this photograph are Bella, Ida, an unidentified child, and Florence with their parents. Photograph courtesy of Sharlot Hall Museum

The following are excerpts from "Fireless Cooking: The Hay Box and Its Uses," one of the most fascinating newspaper articles pasted in the scrapbook of Nellie von Gerichten Smith, wife of Barney Smith who owned the Palace Saloon in Prescott.

Preparing Meals Without Fuel: Though the method is old — almost a century old (circa 1880s) it is said — yet "fireless cookery," brought up to date, may be new to many, and a brief description of how it is accomplished will doubtless be welcome.

Our great-grandmothers and grandmothers used the hay box in the "old country," and in the armies of the continent this same method of fireless cookery has been used with success for many years. Progressive American housewives are now adopting it and enthusiastically sounding its praises.

The primitive "hay box" has evolved into the "asbestos box" and the "copper, double-tank cooker," but while the modern improvements have added greatly to the expense of the original, they have done very little, if anything, to further the practicability of the work which the unpretentious invention of our ancestors accomplished. The latter can be made right at home, without any expense, by any handy man or woman, in the following manner:

Secure or make a box, about the size and shape of a trunk with casters under it so its easy to move, and hinge a snug fitting cover to it. If you can spare a trunk, all the better, as that will save you the work of making the box and cover. In any case, whether it is a box or trunk, see to it that there are no open cracks (if there are, fill them) and then line the inside and cover with thick paper (newsprint is good), pasting it in, and generously overlapping all seams. In short, get it absolutely airtight. If you can afford to line it with asbestos, all the better, but asbestos is not essential. Next pack in, three-quarters full, finely cut, clean, sweet-smelling hay, as closely as you can. Never use coarse or clover hay. Make a ticking pillow stuffed with hay and covered with a muslin slip, to fit as an inside cover, before the top wooden cover is clapped down. Be sure to have the pillow large enough, and well and evenly stuffed — about 5 or 6 inches thick. Now, all you need after that are two or three earthen, iron, or granite-ware kettles or cook pots, with tightly fitting covers, and you are ready for business.

If your hay box is large, divide it by wooden partitions and line them with heavy paper, as well. For cleanliness and to help the hay nests retain their shape, line them with muslin. Hollow out neat "nests" in the hay, into which the cook pots will just fit snugly up to the top, and after you have cooked the contents of the pot over the fire the required number of minutes, according to the recipes for each dish, remove the pots to the hay box nests immediately, without lifting the covers, and quickly put over the hay pillow, clap down the cover, cover the whole box with an old, clean carpet, a shawl or coat, or an old quilt, and put heavy weights on top to prevent warping from steam. Your soup, or meat, or stew, or whatever you have put in, will keep right on cooking, until you open the box again.

Methods and Results: The principle is simple enough: when anything has once reached the boiling point, all that is needed is to keep it there and this is accomplished by depositing the boiling, bubbling food in the covered kettle in an air-tight receptacle which will retain the heat. This is what the hay box does. The first cooking or boiling over a fire takes only from 2 to 5 minutes and can be done over a stove in the early morning. Remember, the hay box cooks or stews — it does not roast or fry. Also, the hay box cooks more slowly than the fire, requiring double the time, but it does it better, and more thoroughly, retaining the juices and aroma, which make the food more wholesome and palatable. Care must be taken to keep the hay and pillow clean and sweet-smelling. It is necessary to renew the hay once a month, and you can save hay by using a layer of tightly crumpled newspaper in the bottom of the box. Some hay box devotees prefer small, separate hay boxes for each cook pot, and perhaps the beginner would do well to try that scheme first.

A Few Cooking Suggestions: Rice, oatmeal or other cereals need a start of 5 minutes cooking over a fire. If wanted for breakfast, can remain in hay box all night. Food cooked in hay box never burns and never gets over done.

Pot roast should first be browned or seared over the fire, then cooked about 20 minutes before putting in hay box, where it should remain about 4 hours. Treat chicken the same, but if it is old, leave longer in hay box.

For baked beans, soak overnight, parboil, mix and boil 10 minutes, then put in hay box at least 6 hours. Take out and brown in oven.

Soups and stews, after a good start over the fire, should have from 6 to 8 hours in the hay box. Vegetables require only 2 to 3 hours in the box — potatoes a little longer.

Some of Its Advantages: It is so nice to come home from church and find the Sunday dinner all ready to serve, or be able to leave a hot, well-cooked dinner for the hungry men-folks when we want to go visiting. Being able to do so encourages us to "take a day off" oftener. It is so nice to be able to cook a dinner for company a day beforehand, and so be free from care and able to enjoy their visit. It may not be generally known that so long as the food is left undisturbed, it will keep several days — in fact, vegetables that sour easily in hot weather will keep a week in the hay box undisturbed (put in boiling, of course). It follows, of course, that a meal is never spoiled by waiting when cooked in a hay stove.

It is a wonderful help to the mother of several little "early risers" to know that the coffee, cereal and various other things are all ready, and dressing the children doesn't delay the breakfast. Then it's a great saver of fuel and the food is so much better cooked that it not only tastes better, but digests better also. One can have hot water for a tub bath hours after all fires are out by putting the kettle in the hay box, and milk or water can be kept warm all night for a baby in a little box made just for the purpose. Also, dinner can be got ready while cooking breakfast, and the whole forenoon spent in the garden.

Hay Box Recipes: The time required for cooking is given, but things requiring only 2 hours can be put in with others requiring 8 or 10 hours, so the box need not be disturbed, as long standing does not spoil anything in the least. Whatever is cooked in the hay box requires at least twice as long cooking as over the fire. Plenty of water must be put in at the start for all dried foods that swell — beans, cereals, dried fruits, etc. — and no water allowed for evaporation with the other sorts.

Peas

Boil 10 minutes on the stove, add milk to cover, butter, salt and pepper to season, bring to a boil again and put into the hay box for 2 hours.

Asparagus

Break off all tough ends, boil 5 minutes on the stove and place in the hay box for 1 hour. If one likes to use the water in which it is cooked, milk, butter, pepper and salt may be added and it is ready when taken up; otherwise, the water can be drained off when taken up and a cream sauce made over the fire.

Summer Squash

Pare, remove seeds and cut in small pieces, add water and boil 5 minutes on the stove and 2 hours in the hay box. Drain, mash, season with butter, salt, pepper, and a little cream if liked.

Beets

Wash, and boil 10 minutes on the stove. Place in the hay box for 2 hours. Slip off skins, chop fine, and season generously with butter and pepper, also add some sugar and salt, and either ½ cup sweet cream or a little vinegar, as preferred, but don't add both cream and vinegar.

Nearly all desserts will cook in 2 hours in the hay box, but it does not follow that they cannot be put in until 2 hours before wanted, as they remain hot a long time and can be left in all day if that is most convenient.

Rice Pudding

1 quart milk
1 to 3 cups rice
1 to 3 cups sugar, depending on
    desired sweetness

1 tablespoon butter
½ teaspoon salt
1 grated rind of lemon

Put milk, rice and sugar, butter, salt and the grated rind of a lemon or other flavoring, into a deep pudding pan. Bring the milk to boiling, set the pan in a kettle of boiling water, let boil 5 minutes and remove to the hay box without removing the lid. Leave in 3 hours or longer. Each grain will be whole and separate, but soft as jelly.

Brown Betty

1½ cups fine breadcrumbs
2 cups minced tart apples
½ teaspoon cinnamon

½ teaspoon allspice
3 well-beaten eggs

Mix breadcrumbs with tart apples. Add cinnamon, allspice, and eggs, and turn into a buttered pudding dish. Set in a kettle of boiling water and cook on the fire 20 minutes and in the hay box 3 hours. Serve with any preferred liquid sauce.

Note: By adding sugar, milk and butter, this pudding might be improved.

Dried Fruit Sauce

First wash well and then soak peaches, apples, prunes, pears or apricots overnight in cold water. In the morning add sugar according to the kind of fruit, boil 5 minutes then set in the hay box 2 hours. Or, the sugar may be omitted and boiled to a syrup separately and added after the fruit is cooked.

Rolled Beefsteak

Steak cut about ½ inch thick
1 pint dressing made from
   breadcrumbs, melted butter,
   salt, pepper, and poultry
   seasoning or sweet herbs

½ cup drippings
2 tablespoons flour
1 pint water
Salt and pepper to taste

Cut out the bone from a steak that is cut about ½-inch thick. Spread the meat with dressing. Press the dressing down smoothly, roll and wrap securely with twine. Put drippings into a heavy skillet and when quite hot lay in the roll and turn it until browned all around. Lift into a kettle and add flour to the remaining grease; when browned add water, salt and pepper to season, and when it has boiled, pour it over the beef roll in the kettle. Start the meat to boiling briskly in the gravy, then remove, closely covered, to the hay box and leave for 5 or 6 hours. Lift to a hot platter, add a little grated onion to the gravy and pour it over the loaf.

Old Chicken Fried

With the aid of the hay box one can have fried chicken any morning for breakfast, even from the oldest hen on the place. Joint, add boiling water to cover, salt to season, and boil 15 minutes. Put in the hay box overnight. In the morning, drain out the pieces, roll in flour, and fry brown. Use the broth in making the gravy.

Boiled Dinner

Put the ham or corned beef in first and boil ½ hour. Then add cabbage, onions, turnips, carrots, potatoes or whatever assortment of vegetables is liked. Let all boil again for 10 minutes, then put in the hay box for 4 to 6 hours.

Note: You may have been using this labor-saving device all along; it is known to modern homemakers as a "crock pot."

In July 1879 Miss Nellie Cashman opened Delmonico's Restaurant on the south side of Church Plaza in Tucson. George Whitwell Parsons, on his way to the rich strikes at Tombstone in February 1880, made this entry in his journal for Tuesday, the 10th: "Lunch basket getting low — so tried restaurant for breakfast and had an excellent one at Delmonico's on Camp Street. Kept by two Irish girls — good and clean. Four bits (fifty cents) a meal. Very reasonable for the place and what you get. It was amusing to hear her ask in gentle tones what we'd have and thunder the order in stentorian voice at the Mexican cook."

The stories of the Tombstone boom enticed Nellie to relocate and she opened a hotel and restaurant at the corner of Fifth and Toughnut streets. Through wise investments, she also acquired a grocery store and saloon, but she was best known for her personal kindnesses and public generosity. Through her efforts, St. Mary's Hospital was opened in Tucson. It was run by the Sisters of St. Joseph and was the first non-military, public hospital in the territory. In July 1881 she brought three of the Sisters of Mercy to Tombstone to run the local hospital there. Often her own hotel doubled as a charity hospital with Nellie as nurse. She was instrumental in building one of the first schools in Tombstone, and through her efforts to secure donations, as well as a large personal contribution, Tombstone's first Catholic church was built. Many of her fund raising drives received generous donations from the saloons and brothels which did a thriving business in the boomtown.

Although she made a great deal of money, it was always used to help those down on their luck. Nellie became known as the "Angel of the Camp," and whenever she entered a room, every man present stood up. One miner, whom she had befriended, overheard a traveling salesman complaining about Nellie's beans. Quietly he walked over to the stranger and suggested that the drummer try the beans again. Perhaps eating with a cocked revolver at his head added just the right seasoning, for he declared them delicious after all.

In 1883, at the death of her sister, "Aunt Nell" took over the care and education of her three nieces and two nephews, who ranged in age from twelve to four. The boys loved to play baseball, but often a dispute would mar the end of the game so Aunt Nell would call in both teams and serve big slices of pie all around. Nellie's intervention did not teach them fair play and sportsmanship; the fights continued on a regular basis and soon every game ended with pie at Nellie Cashman's Restaurant.

By 1893 one of her nephews, Mike Cunningham, had moved to Prescott and was employed in the office of the Yavapai County District Attorney. Aunt Nell came to visit and five years later returned to open the Arizona Silver Belt Restaurant in Prescott. Here she renewed her acquaintance with Ephilet B. Gage, whose life she had saved when he was superintendent of the Grand Central Mining Company in Tombstone. Gage made a fortune in that boomtown and never forgot the buggy ride provided by Nellie which spirited him away to the safety of Tucson, just ahead of strikers who planned to kidnap and hang him because he would not give in to unreasonable demands.

Among Nellie's other admirer's were Wyatt Earp, "Doc" Holliday, John P. Clum, who was editor of the Tombstone Epitaph, Ed Schieffelin who found rich silver strikes instead of the tombstone supposedly awaiting him for intruding into Apache territory, and Sam Lee who worked as Nellie's cook and took her photograph with him when he visited his home in China so that this portrait of Nell could be painted by an artist in Hong Kong.

Descendants of Nellie Cashman continue to live in Arizona. Photograph courtesy of the Department of Library, Archives and Public Records, State of Arizona

Pie Paste (crust)

½ pound (2 sticks) butter   1 pound (4 cups) flour
¼ pound lard   Cold water or milk to mix

Combine butter and lard; add flour, mixing with pastry cutter or fork. Add enough cold water or milk to moisten. Roll out thin on lightly floured board, then carefully transfer to pie tin and cut away excess. Prick with fork then bake at 400 degrees F. for 15 to 20 minutes if it's to be filled with prepared filling.

~✄~

Special Pie Crust

2 cups melted lard   Flour as needed
1 cup cold water

Combine hot lard with 1 cup cold water and, immediately, enough flour to make a stiff dough. Do this right after breakfast and set it away. By the time the dishes are washed, the crust is cool. More flour can then be kneaded in, if necessary, and pies made. Roll out and bake in a quick oven (425 degrees F. for 8 to 10 minutes or until golden).

Blueberry Pie

Line plates with pie paste (unbaked), sprinkle with 3 heaping tablespoons sugar, fill rounding full with blueberries, dot with a little butter, cover with an upper crust, and bake until berries are cooked (425 degrees F. for 50 minutes or until crust is golden). If swamp blueberries are used in any of these recipes, more sugar will be required, as the berries aren't as sweet as high ground berries. Always use granulated sugar, as it is much sweeter than the powdered.

Cherry Pie

Pitted cherries
½ cup sugar

1 tablespoon flour
Bits of butter

Line a pie tin with a good crust (unbaked), fill with pitted cherries, sweeten with sugar, and sprinkle over it flour and bits of butter, if liked. Cover with a top crust and bake slowly (425 degrees F. for 50 minutes or until golden).

Sweet Potato Pie

Yield: One large or two medium pies

1 to 2 sweet potatoes
1 tablespoon butter
2 well-beaten eggs
2 cups milk

1 cup shredded coconut
Grated rind and juice of 1 lemon
Sugar to taste
Dash cinnamon and nutmeg

Boil sweet potatoes until soft and mash fine while hot; add butter, eggs, milk, shredded coconut, grated rind and juice of lemon, and sugar to taste, with a dash of cinnamon and nutmeg, if liked. Bake with a rich undercrust (400 degrees F. for 10 minutes and 325 degrees F. for 30 minutes).

Banana Cream Pie

Bananas, as needed
2 egg yolks
2 tablespoons sugar

1 teaspoon orange extract
1½ cups rich milk

Meringue
2 egg whites, stiffly beaten
2 heaping teaspoons sugar

Line a deep pie plate with a crust and rim and fill with thin slices of banana. Beat the yolk of eggs with sugar; add orange extract, and rich milk; pour over the bananas and bake like custard; then cover with meringue; brown lightly in the oven.

Lemon Pie

1 heaping tablespoon butter
3 cups milk
3 level tablespoons cornstarch

Little cold water or milk
Juice and grated rind of 1 lemon
Sugar to taste

Line a pie tin with a good crust and bake. When wanted, fill with the following mixture: boil together butter, milk, and cornstarch dissolved in a little cold water or milk. Boil until it thickens, then remove from fire, stir in juice and grated rind of lemon, and sugar. Fill the pie crust and serve when cold.

Chocolate Pie

1 cup sweet milk
1 scant cup plus 3 tablespoons
  sugar
3 tablespoons grated bitter

chocolate
2 eggs, separated
3 level tablespoons of flour
1 teaspoon vanilla extract

Boil sweet milk and one scant cup sugar. When very hot add chocolate and stir until dissolved. Have the yolks of eggs beaten light and flour mixed smooth with a little milk. Stir these ingredients together and gradually beat into the boiling milk. Stir constantly until it is thick. When cool add vanilla and pour into a previously baked crust. Beat the whites of eggs until peaks stand alone, then add 3 tablespoons sugar, beat again, and pour over the pie. Set in a hot oven to brown.

Rhubarb Pie

Boiling water, as needed
2 cups chopped rhubarb
(Add sweetners to taste)
1 egg

1 tablespoon butter
1 tablespoon flour
3 tablespoons water
3 tablespoons sugar

Pour boiling water over chopped rhubarb and drain off the water after 5 minutes, then mix yolk of egg, butter, and flour, moistening the whole with water. Bake with a lower crust only (425 degrees F. for 40 to 50 minutes). Make a meringue of the white of the egg and sugar, spread over the top of the pie and return to the oven to brown.

John B. Allen had acquired a number of talents by age thirty-nine, but getting rich with a pick and shovel wasn't one of them! He was penniless when he joined the gold rush along the lower Gila River in the late 1850s, and his luck held. While others struck it rich, he left as destitute as he had come. But he soon earned a reputation in Calabazas, Tubac, Tombstone, and Tucson by offering something any dusty desert rat would pay a dollar for: a golden-crusted, sweetly spicy, downright delectable dried apple pie.

"Pie" Allen's business prospered, and he purchased one hundred sixty acres at Maricopa Wells where he grew hay and became the only merchant on the stage line between Yuma and Tucson. His ranching and farming activities expanded rapidly, and he opened several mercantile stores in Tubac, Tombstone, and Tucson. Because of his popularity, "Pie" Allen was elected to the territorial legislature, later served as territorial treasurer, served two terms as mayor of Tucson, and when he was appointed adjutant general in the mid-1870s he became known as General "Pie" Allen.

Like many other prospectors, he never discovered that bonanza of gold nuggets. Instead he found his fortune hidden in a golden-crusted pie pan.

In 1867 Prescott lost the territorial capital to Tucson, then a village with a wall about ten feet high built by the Spanish in 1776 as protection against Indian attack. The town well supplied water which was drawn in the morning for that day's use. Almost every house had a burro-powered stone grinder for the wheat and corn used in preparing tortillas. Canned goods were five dollars per can and soap sold for one dollar a bar. Chilies dried in the sun by each doorway and desert bees drowsed in the squash blossoms. The imprint of the Spanish and Mexican occupation was clearly visible in every aspect of dress, diet and architecture. But by March 20, 1880, when the railroad arrived, the community was an odd and lively mixture of "Spanican" and "Yankee." Adobe buildings now housed watchmakers and photo galleries. At the end of the 1880s Tucson boasted such modern conveniences as telephone service, gas and electric lights, and running water.

Shown here are views of Tucson in 1880 (above) and 1885 (below). Photographs courtesy of the Department of Library, Archives and Public Records, State of Arizona

By March of 1880 George Whitwell Parsons had established himself in Tombstone. He shared a house with several other miners but it had only a roof, four walls, and a dirt floor. He was often kept awake by rats skittering back and forth, and the wind and cold night temperatures were bone chilling. George enjoyed being self-sufficient and noted in his journal that he prepared almost all his own meals. Lunch was usually a slab of ham slapped between two slabs of equally heavy bread, then stuffed unceremoniously into one of his front pants pockets until mealtime.

The glamour of setting out for the silver fields paled considerably under the southern Arizona sun. On Thursday, March 18, 1880 Parsons wrote: "Some nerve required to hold hands just under the pound of the hammer. One little slip and one's hands, arms or legs might be smashed to jelly." On Wednesday, March 31, he confided: "My poor hands and arms are in terrible state. I suffer much but grin and bear it. This is a trial I venture to say that very, very few of my condition in life have ever experienced. I've roughed it before — worked hard and endured much physically — but *this* beats it all. Why, even these rough miners themselves — men used to manual labor all their lives — are sometimes laid up for weeks at a time when they first try the mines. This is something before which all former experiences pale. Kinney says he don't want to discourage me but is afraid I won't be able to stand it. I'll show him."

And so he did. Kinney "complimented me today saying partner (a great word here)," and Parson boasted "I now have what is called my wind. Can sling a sledge all the afternoon — can strike a hundred blows without stopping."

George Whitwell Parsons was a rather well-to-do young man of thirty when he decided to forsake his nightly game of whist in the salons of San Francisco and try his hand at striking it rich in the silver fields of Tombstone. In his Tuesday, February 3, 1880 journal entry he stated that his "outfit" consisted of:

2 pairs double blankets — 4 prints	$13.00
1 rubber blanket	2.00
rubber pillow	3.25
rubber leggings	1.25
rubber cap (soft)	.35
cork screw	.35
miner's shirt (3)	4.50
riveted overalls	1.85
duck cover for pillow	.75
and sundries — F shirts — drawers	
WC (Authors note: water closet) paper — tooth brush	
paper collar and cuffs — bone studs	
trunk strap — blacking	
stationary and clothes repaired	6.75
making total of	34.05
Ticket through to Tucson	57.50

Grand total $91.55
$7.00 to Tombstone and necessary expenses
at Tucson will make amount over $100 —
considerable

On February 4 he encountered his first problem: "Lively times today. Had to get Mrs. H, Mrs. Mc, S and C to stand on trunk when I tried to fasten it."

Bachelor's Bread

2 cups sour milk
1 heaping teaspoon baking soda
Salt to taste
2 tablespoons sugar
1 egg

2 tablespoons butter or lard
½ cup flour
Cornmeal and graham flour, as
   needed

To sour milk add soda, a little salt, sugar, egg, butter or lard, and flour. Add equal parts of cornmeal and graham flour to make a stiff batter. Bake 40 minutes in a moderate over (350 degrees F.). Serve hot.

This photograph shows ten of Bisbee, Arizona's mine workers, taken before the Copper Queen Mine was wired with electricity. Each miner carried a pointed candle holder with a sharp point so he could stick it in the timbers where he was working. Men carried their lunches in tin buckets; the ones with cups had a compartment where they carried coffee. Heavy red flannel shirts were worn to protect the men, since they came up from hot mines dripping wet. In the very early days, change rooms were not available, and the miners had to walk to their homes in their wet clothes. Left to right are John Barnin, Bill Campbell, Bert Gnohlun, John Pennypaker, Jack Trizise, Frank Johnson, Andy Lidigiust, Jim Allison, John True, and Charles Beackburm. Photograph courtesy of the Department of Library, Archives and Public Records, State of Arizona

This hotel in Globe was indeed international, from its white washed adobe walls to the calico-capped chambermaid. Like many establishments of its kind, it catered to a wide variety of clientele as both a hotel and a restaurant.

The half dozen men on the far left seem to be an assortment of employees, business men, and perhaps a prospector or two. The woman to the left of the chambermaid appears to be quite confidently holding a cigarette. Could she have been a "bloomer girl," an emancipated female who wore that indecent, unmentionable undergarment, was known to go brasless, to smoke and to drink, and was suspected of even darker deeds? The man, young child, woman, and dog to the right may be a family group.

Public facilities offered throughout Arizona were becoming standardized by the 1890s, and while they were still somewhat less than luxurious, they offered security and sustenance to the lonely bachelor and weary traveler. The food was simply prepared, amply provided, and an interesting mixture of the provisions available and the ethnic background of the cook. Photograph courtesy of the Department of Library, Archives and Public Records, State of Arizona

Mulligatawney Soup

2 rabbits
¼ pound (1 stick) butter
Sliced onions

3 pints clear soup stock
Flour and butter, as needed
Juice of lemon

Have rabbits cut in pieces; fry them in butter with some sliced onions. When done put into clear soup stock and boil for an hour. Strain this and mash the onions through a sieve. Add more broth if needed, and boil for another hour. Make a smooth paste of flour and butter and add this to thicken the broth; when well mixed put in the juice of a lemon and simmer a while longer.

German Egg Noodles

½ cup flour
Pinch salt

1 egg, beaten

Add flour and salt to the beaten egg, forming a soft dough. Place on a floured bread board and knead until the dough loses its stickiness. Roll out paper thin, about 12 to 14 inches in diameter. Let stand covered at least twenty minutes, then sprinkle the dough with additional flour and roll it up, jelly-roll fashion. Slice into ¼-inch-wide pieces with a sharp knife. Sprinkle with more flour as needed to separate the little rolls and set them aside to dry. (Drop into boiling salted water and cook until tender.)

— Leona J. Gray,
Granddaughter of Eulalia and E. G. Frankenberg, Jr.

This recipe was a favorite of the Frankenberg family. Ernst George Frankenburg, Jr. reached the Salt River Valley on December 19, 1888 and settled on a tract of wild desert land near Tempe, where he began raising livestock and farming. E. G. Frankenburg, Jr. served as director of the Tempe Irrigating Canal Company, president of the Farmers and Merchants Bank, director of the Bank of Tempe, and supervisor for Maricopa County. His descendants still live in Tempe.

Potato Salad

Yield: 4 to 6 Servings

1 quart cold boiled potatoes, chopped
1 small onion, chopped

1 stalk celery, chopped
2 sprigs parsley, minced fine
1 hard-cooked egg, chopped

Dressing
2 teaspoons flour
2 teaspoons sugar
1 teaspoon salt
½ teaspoon mustard

¼ teaspoon black pepper
1 cup vinegar
2 eggs, well-beaten
1 cup sweet cream

Combine potatoes, onion, celery, parsley and egg in a serving dish. Add dressing and gently mix until vegetables are thoroughly coated.

In a small saucepan, mix dressing ingredients well together and boil till thickened. Remove from heat and add eggs slowly while beating. When cold add cream. Without the cream, this dressing will keep in a cool place one week.

German Dressing

½ cup thick cream
¼ teaspoon salt

Pepper to taste
3 tablespoons vinegar

Beat cream until stiff with an egg beater. Add salt, pepper, and vinegar very slowly, beating continuously.

Toad in the Hole

This is an English dish and a good one despite its unpleasant name.

1 pound round steak
1 to 2 eggs
1 pint milk
1 cup flour

½ teaspoon baking powder
½ teaspoon salt
Salt, pepper, and sage to taste

Cut steak into pieces about 1 inch square. Make a smooth batter of eggs, milk, flour, baking powder, and salt. Butter a pudding dish; place the meat in the dish and season well with salt, pepper, and sage. Pour over it the batter, leaving some of the larger meat cubes with their "heads" stuck out. Bake 30 to 45 minutes at about 400 degrees F., or until crust is goldren brown and a broom straw or knife comes out clean. Serve hot.

Note: This can also be made with mutton, lamb, or pork.

Scotch Short Bread

1¾ pounds (6 to 7 cups) pastry flour
¼ pound (about 1 cup) rice flour

1 pound (4 sticks) butter, at room temperature
½ pound sugar

Sift together pastry and rice flours. Cream butter with sugar and then gradually work in flour mixture. Blend until smooth, spread in shallow tins about 1 inch thick, and bake in a moderate oven (350 degrees F. for 35 to 40 minutes or until bread tests done).

Toast:

Here's to old St. Patrick
With strategy and stealth
He drove the snakes from Ireland
Here's a bumper to his health.
But not too many bumpers
Lest we exceed and then
Forget the dear old gentlemen
And see the snakes again.

Contributed by
Gail Gardner

Even before the territorial legislature convened for the first time, native beer was being served in Prescott. A Sunday school, a church, a hospital, a library — all were established only after the basic needs of the pioneer population had been met. The first saloon, the Quartz Rock, opened on the banks of Granite Creek to be near the gold claims. Its entire operation consisted of a plank for a bar, two bottles of whiskey and a communal cup, served up by a noseless army deserter. But the very creek which provided the Quartz Rock revenue proved to be its biggest drawback as well. Due, no doubt, to the potency of the potions served there, more patrons were making it into the creek than were making it across. So the Quartz Rock was moved to a new location on Montezuma, where a number of other saloons were opened and the whole street dubbed "Whiskey Row." Across the Plaza on Cortez Street, Tom Hodges ran one of the first well-regulated saloons. He sold drinks and cigars, taking gold nuggets and burros in payment.

The saloon was much more than just a place to drink. It usually offered a variety of inducements including sleeping rooms, facilities for bathing and getting a shave, and the latest news. Court, church services, political debates, sporting events, and every sort of entertainment from seductive singing to classical concerts were held here. As can be seen in this photograph of the Owl Saloon, it also served as a natural history museum and art gallery. John S. Ross is shown standing by the cash register with Mr. Bagsby to the right.

It is as a social club that saloons are most often thought of. And if it hadn't been for the civilizing influence of "hurdy-gurdy" girls, men would never have given up spitting on the floor or taken up bathing. When there weren't enough girls to go around for dancing, prospectors, soldiers, and cowboys would tie a handkerchief around their right arms to indicate they were the females and would follow. Favorite dances included the cross-eyed snap, Irishman's trot, and Do-Si-Do. Of course, the purpose of all this exertion was not just to entertain the patrons but to encourage them in working up a thirst. "Ladies of the evening" also urged the men to drink, and the salt-laden "free lunch" made it almost impossible to refuse. For five cents a customer could buy a glass of beer and a sandwich of his choice; ten cents purchased a stein and all he could eat. The spread varied but was sure to include highly seasoned foods guaranteed to produce thirst.

Unfortunately, saloons offered ample opportunity to appease man's baser drives as well. Prostitution and gambling were often a town's best-paid professions, drunkenness was ignored, and the brew was so raw that one of the fires which Tombstone experienced (June 1881) was reputed to have been caused by a keg of whiskey blowing up. In late 1864 or early 1865, Lois and Ed Boblett rented a house on Montezuma Street (about where Matt's is today), and according to Mrs. Boblett in her journal:

"There was a saloon and bowling alley adjoining it but no door was to open between. One day two men got in a fight and one was beating the other over the head with an iron pin and to get away he burst down the door and came into our part of the house. Everything went on fine for a while until one night they commenced shooting in the saloon and some of the shots came in our part, into the dining room, and of all the yelling and smashing of windows, I never heard before or since, and hope I never shall again. I and the children were terribly frightened so Ed took us to a neighbor's till the row was over. Then there were a lot of soldiers who come up from the post and, for some reason, were mad at Mr. Holiday, the saloon keeper, and they had come on purpose to bust up everything. They were not aiming to do us any damage but some of them got so drunk they did not know what they were doing so they began to throw cord wood through our dining room window. One rather large stick was thrown on one of the tables that was all set and broke several dishes. Ed took his gun then and I think he would have shot, only some of the sober ones came and took them away telling us they did not want to destroy things of ours for we had nothing to do with the saloon part of the house. They kept on in the saloon till they broke everything Mr. Holiday had, even to chairs, and poured out all of his liquor so they had to leave and we were very glad for then we had quietness." Photograph courtesy of Sharlot Hall Museum

Scholey Beans

This was served at Scholey and Stephans Saloon as part of their free lunch.

Yield: Feeds at least a dozen hungry men

1 quart dried red beans
½ pound salt pork
1 large onion, cut fine
1 cup lard or other cooking fat
Salt to taste

½ pound round steak
1 can green chilies
1 small piece garlic
Several red dried Mexican Chili peppers

Wash and clean beans. Soak overnight in warm water. In a 10-quart kettle, combine beans, salt pork, onion, and lard; cook until beans begin to get tender. Cook red chili peppers in a small amount of water until tender. Work them through a colander. Fry round steak in its own suet or small pieces of suet. When well done, put the meat through a meat grinder. Add garlic, red chilies, green chilies, and ground meat to the beans. Cook over low heat, allowing plenty of time for flavors to mingle.

Ham and Pickle Sandwiches

Chop cold boiled ham very fine, using a meat chopper if you have it. Mix to a good consistency for spreading with melted butter, mustard, and finely chopped cucumber pickles; spread between thin slices of bread and butter.

Rye Bread

1 quart rye
1 pint wheat flour
1½ pints milk
½ compressed yeast cake

Lard the size of an egg
½ cup sugar
1 teaspoon salt

To rye add wheat flour, milk, and yeast. Into the flour, rub the lard, sugar, and salt. Mold and set aside to rise overnight. In the morning mold again, put into greased pans, and let rise. Bake at 375 degrees F. for 1 hour or until golden.

Saratoga Crisps

Slice the potatoes wafer thin and evenly, dropping into cold water to crisp. Let them lie a half hour, then drain and pat dry in a soft cloth. Have ready a kettle of boiling lard, and drop in the potatoes a few at a time. As fast as they rise to the surface crisp and brown, remove them with a skimmer, shaking off extra fat. Lay them on soft paper to absorb any grease remaining. Sprinkle with salt and set in a dry place until ready to serve.

Pickled Eggs

Hard-cooked eggs
1 quart of vinegar
1 tablespoon mustard
1 teaspoon salt

½ teaspoon pepper
½ dozen cloves
1 dozen allspice

Place shelled hard-cooked eggs in a crock and pour over them vinegar in which has been boiled mustard, salt, pepper, cloves, and allspice.

Note: Sometimes the salt is omitted and a stick of cinnamon added.

Pickled Beets

Young red beets
1 quart vinegar

1 pound sugar

Select nice young red beets and boil until tender. Plunge them from the boiling into cold water for a minute or two, until the peel will slip off readily by just rubbing them with your fingers. Boil together vinegar and sugar for 5 minutes, and then put in the beets cut in quarter pieces (only enough beets to fill one can at a time) and let them boil for a minute or two, after which skim them out, pour into cans, fill up with the syrup, and seal.

Dill Pickles

Make a brine strong enough to bear an egg, then add half as much more water as you have brine. Wash the cucumbers in cold water, and into a stone jar put first a layer of cucumbers, then a layer of grape leaves, and a layer of dill, using leaves and stems. Continue in this way until the jar is full. Pour the brine over all, and cover, first with a cloth, then with a plate, and put a weight on top of the plate. The cloth must be taken off and washed frequently, as in making sauerkraut.

To Make Sauerkraut

Cut up cabbage in very fine slices. Take a small, clean barrel, put in a layer of cabbage, and spread over it a couple of handfuls of salt, then a layer of cabbage, salt, etc. until the barrel is full. Press each layer down well, and at last there will be a brine which should cover the cabbage. Cover (inside) with a clean white cloth, over this place a round piece of board to fit inside, and on top of it a clean, heavy stone, so that the kraut will stay under the brine. After some weeks it will ferment and then be ready for use. When taking a portion out of the barrel, remove stone and board and cloth very carefully, and give each a thorough cleaning before returning to its place. Also remove any scum which clings to the side and top of the barrel. Keep in a cool, dry place.

To Cook It

If it is very sour, wash it in fresh, cold water. Wring it out in a ball with your hands, and spread lightly in an agate cooking vessel. Add very little salt and water and a tablespoon of lard, cover closely, and let boil slowly for 1 hour. A piece of not too strong salt pork can be added instead of the fresh lard, in which case the salt is of course omitted. Serve hot with potatoes and roast pork.

If a man came west and struck it rich or established a cattle empire or built a railroad or was elected mayor, his family shared in his good fortune. But not all of the inhabitants of the Arizona territory were so nobly inclined. People brought their highest ideals and their petty meannesses west with them, and sometimes a man's wrongdoings not only caused his family to suffer but forced them to share his fate. Such was the case with the Dilda family.

This photograph of Dennis Dilda with his wife Georgia and their children, five-year-old Fern and ten-month-old John, was taken by Erwin Baer on January 2, 1886 in the jailor's room of the Yavapai County courthouse in Prescott. Dilda was waiting to be hung for the cold-blooded murder of Deputy Sheriff John M. Murphy, and Georgia was being held because she helped him bury the body. Since there was no one to take care of the children, they stayed in the cell with her. Local newspapers revealed that Dilda had killed a man in Georgia, one in Texas, one in New Mexico, and three in the Salt River Valley — including his wife's brother. She had come from a good Phoenix family named Patterson and was unaware of her husband's unsavory past, although she learned to fear him enough to do as she was told. She and the children were later released and returned to her family's ranch.

About nine in the morning, of February 5, 1886, the condemned man's last meal was brough to him from Ben Butler's Chop House, located in the Palace Saloon. He ate heartily of breaded spring chicken, cream sauce, fried oysters, lamb chops, green peas, tenderloin steak, mushrooms, English pan cake with jelly, potatoes, bread, and coffee. At two that afternoon "Mad Dog" Dilda was brought out of the jail and placed in a barouche by Sheriff Mulvenon and Chief of Police Dodson. Their carriage was escorted by the Prescott Rifles and Prescott Grays up West Gurley Street to the scaffold in a grove of pine trees off what is today Willow Street.

The procession which followed consisted of wagon loads of dance hall girls and local citizens. Henry Hartin's father, who had come to Prescott as a farrier with the army and eventually opened his own blacksmith shop, had forbidden Henry to attend the hanging, but the lad went anyway. The militia formed a square around the scaffold, and from the back of the grove came the strains of piano music played by John Marion's wife, Flora. Dilda took a long swig of whiskey, was hooded, and the rope placed around his neck. Just as the trap door flew open, Hartin snatched Henry away and hauled him home. "Bucky" O'Neill, a member of the Prescott Grays, fainted and was caught by Dick McNary.

It was just such lawlessness — as well as the harshness of frontier justice — that caused the women to strengthen their efforts in bringing social and cultural advancement to Arizona. Their concept of what a community should be was much different than the society sought by men. Photograph courtesy of Sharlot Hall Museum

This unidentified health seeker is enjoying Castle Creek hot springs about 1900, four years after it opened as a resort and spa for the well-to-do. Photograph courtesy of Sharlot Hall Museum

Home Remedies

The Indians understood and benefitted from the curative properties of the hot springs in the high desert southeast of present day Wickenburg long before their "discovery" by Anglos. In 1873 George Monroe and his common-law wife, Mollie Sawyer, were coming up Castle Creek one rainy afternoon. Mollie got off her horse and leaned over to take a drink of the clear waters, but it was so hot that she spat it out, then screamed, "Hell isn't half a mile from this place. Let's get out of here, George."

First calling it Monroe Springs, George and Mollie built a cabin out of cane but did not live on their claim. In May 1877 Jesse Jackson and S. Rood of Prescott jumped the Monroe claim. In their group were two men named Carpenter and Wheeler who accompanied Jackson and Rood for the sole purpose of using the spring's health-giving waters. On June 16, 1877 the *Enterprise* published a letter sent out on pack train enroute to Wickenburg. The men gave this report:

> This region is but little known, even to the oldest prospectors in this country, although lying almost in the heart of the richest mining district of the territory. Our place is situated about sixty miles south of Prescott and about twenty miles south of the Peck mine. Provisions are getting scarce —plenty of beans and venison but flour and bacon are running light.

> The waters of these springs are known to contain valuable medical properties from our own experience. Two of our party, Carpenter and Wheeler, have greatly benefitted their health in a week's bathing. The waters have no disagreeable taste or smell, on the contrary they are pleasant to drink and large quantities can be taken. Being cooled in canteens overnight, it is the purest, most delicious water ever drank. The temperature of the water at the head of the creek is 160 degrees Fahrenheit — at the bathing pool about two hundred yards below, the temperature is reduced fully thirty degrees and at the mouth of Castle Creek it is cool enough to drink. There are no frosts in winter and no extremely hot weather in summer. Deer, rabbitt (sic), and quail abound and our larder has been bountifully supplied since our arrival. The mountains around are thickly covered with a fine growth of Sahauro (sic) cactus twenty to thirty feet high. Their tops are literally covered with beautiful white blossoms which promise well for a bountiful supply of delicious fruit in about ten days. So you see, we have a few of the luxuries even in this country. For health, pleasure, and profit we would advise a visit to the hot springs and a bath in its healing waters.

No claims are made for the effectiveness of any of the home remedies which follow, nor are they meant to replace the advice and skill of a physician. During the early days of the territory, it was necessary for people to treat themselves and their families as best they could simply because doing *something* was better than doing nothing. Even medical doctors realized this fact of life on the frontier as evidenced by an ad run in the *Arizona Miner* of November 7, 1879 in which Doctor George Kendall stated that he had recently received a new shipment of medical supplies and was now "prepared to kill or cure on short notice."

Many remedies were based on Indian lore. Herbs, succulents, and other plants were easily obtainable and used in a variety of ways. Aloe Vera liquid was known to help cuts and wounds, insomnia, stomach disorders, pain, constipation, hemorrhoids, itching, headache, mouth and gum disorders, kidney ailments, sun burns and scalds, ulcers, arthritis, asthma, and much more.

Territorial historian Sharlot Hall observed: "Brave as they were in danger, patient under hardship, ready to make the most of rough surroundings and insufficient means, it was in time of trouble, in sickness and death, that the nobility of the frontier women stands out most strongly. Remote from medical help or from medicines many a woman trained herself to be both nurse and physician, and with simple herbs and homely remedies met as best she could the course of disease and accident."

Often there was seemingly no scientific or medical reason why these remedies were effective, and yet an improvement or cure resulted. Perhaps it was the comforting touch of another human being — the "laying on of hands" referred to in the Bible — which aided the recuperative powers of the patient. A strong desire to ease the pain and anxiety of injury or illness played an important role in the healing process. But sometimes even this was not enough.

According to Sharlot Hall, "No one ever heard of a frontier woman failing to go miles if need be to help another woman in sickness; only a woman who has lived through it can know what sickness on the lonely ranches meant to the women. Many a woman was laid away in a rough grave with her new born babe on her breast for lack of a physician's help and many a mother saw her baby wrapped in a blanket or put into a packing box and hidden under the sand of the desert. It was then that the tenderness of the neighbor who had perhaps driven fifty miles to give what help she could, was felt to the utmost . . . . The neighbor might be an utter stranger but common need in a lonely land made them sisters. One mother, grieving wildly that her first baby must be laid away in a cracker box looked out to see an army ambulance drive up and a strange woman step out. The stranger was the young bride of an army officer on her way to Fort Whipple; among her wedding presents was a big music box in a beautiful rosewood case. She had taken out the mechanism and lined the case with the white silk skirt of her wedding dress and brought the little casket to the mother that she had never seen that the baby might be laid away fittingly."

Mexican Mustang Liniment ad from the scrapbook of Nellie von Gerichten Smith, circa 1880s.

Anna Forbach (shown here) was the wife of Peter Forbach, who owned the trading post on the Sacaton Indian reservation from 1873 until 1881, when they moved to a cattle ranch six miles west of Casa Grande. Mr. Forbach arrived in southern Arizona in 1863 and on April 15, 1871 married Anna. In later years she reminisced: "Mr. Carl [Charles] Hayden, father of the present Congressman Carl Hayden at Washington, had a good eye for business, for when he heard that Peter was to be married, he stored a sewing machine, a fine set of dishes, some ivory handled knives and forks, and a side saddle. He knew Peter would be likely to buy them for his bride."

According to Marie Peters Wells, "Grandmother Anna had two thick Doctor's books and the only way she knew how to help people was to consult her books. A warm climate, food spoiled quickly and dysenteria often [was] the result. They ordered Dr. Peter Farny's Stomach Elixir from Chicago by the case, and [she] saved a good many lives administering it." Photograph courtesy of the Casa Grande Valley Historical Society

Asthma: Drink buttercup tea, or whiskey in mullein tea.

Bruises: Salt applied to a bruise eases the pain; or pound green peach leaves to a pulp and apply.

Dip sliced onion in vinegar and apply at once. Use this often to fade old bruises.

A cloth wrung out in very hot water and often renewed will remove discoloration from bruises.

Carbuncles and Stys: The lining of an eggshell was used in drawing or "bringing to a head" boils or carbuncles.

To cure a sty, use the tail portion of a dead fly and rub it gently on the sty.

Colds and Pneumonia: Drink whiskey with honey for cough.

To relieve congestion of the lungs eat ground lamb's tongue or use a poultice of fried onions or carrot gratings—change when the poultice is no longer warm. Rub hog's grease on chest. Wild cherry bark and berries boiled and flavored with honey or sugar loaf may be used for an expectorant.

A hot, strong lemonade taken at bed time will break up a bad cold.

> Author's Comment: Asafetida, also called Devil's Dung, is the roots of Khizome mixed with other roots. The brownish-yellow mass is the soft, fetid gum resin of various Persian and East Indian plants. It is used in medicine as an antispasmodic and was a common cold medicine, tied in small cloth bags and suspended around the neck to ward off grip, now called influenza, and other communicable diseases. Asafetida had a strong—and, according to Gussie Woods who once wore it, an unforgettable—odor.

Colic: Drink catnip tea with whiskey. Mint tea relieves upsets, cramps and colic.

Mint Tea Recipe

1 teaspoon crushed mint leaves
— fresh or dried

Cover with 1 cup boiling water. Steep five minutes covered. Never boil or it is bittersweet to the taste.

Digestive Upsets: A little baking soda stirred into hot water was the standard remedy for heartburn or sour stomach.

A cup of hot, slightly salted water drunk before meals will relieve nausea and dyspepsia.

To stop vomiting, drink saffron tea.

Arthur Doty Frost and Mabel Leonard Frost left Wyoming in a covered wagon accompanied by her mother and their children, Georgia - age five, James -age three, and Lilian - age one. Two months later, in December 1902, they reached Douglas, Arizona Territory. Arthur Frost worked in the new smelter there, and after his death in 1918, Mabel taught in a number of rural schools and later in the Douglas school system.

This "drawing salve" was made by Mabel Frost and used on insect bites, to help get splinters or thorns out, or to ease inflammations, according to Georgia Frost Newcomer. Her mother mixed equal parts of resin, beeswax, and lard and applied it generously to the affected area. This procedure was followed as long as was necessary to draw out the foreign body, and the salve was used by the Frost descendents until recent years.

Ear Ache: Pour warm urine into the ear. Also tobacco smoke blown into ear will relieve ear ache.

Gently press a bag of heated salt against the outer ear.

Fever: Glycerine and lemon juice, half and half, on a bit of absorbent cotton, is the best thing in the world wherewith to moisten the lips and tongue of a fever-parched patient.

A fever patient can be made cool and comfortable by frequent sponging off with soda water.

Baking powder mixed with lard smeared on the body will reduce fever and soothe aches.

Ora De Concini, mother of Senator Dennis De Concini, remembers that one of the family's home remedies was the external application of a mixture consisting of kerosene and water to cure frostbite.

The first application should be made with cool water. Increase the temperature of the water somewhat with each application by adding tepid water, then warm water to a small amount of kerosene. Never put hot water on frostbite as the skin may not be able to detect the heat and a burn could result. Do not boil the kerosene; mix it with water which has been gradually increased in temperature.

Hands and feet can be soaked in the water-kerosene mixture and it can be applied to other parts of the body with pieces of flannel dipped in the mixture and wrung out. Keep the remedy away from the mouth and eyes.

Headache: Camphor mixed with rye whiskey and rubbed into the scalp.

Two slices from the center of a potato about one half inch thick, soak in vinegar, then place one on each temple.

Inflamed Joints: Use Wintergreen oil to ease inflamed joints.

Insect Bites: Cover an insect bite with a paste of baking soda and water to ease the sting and itching.

A fresh tomato leaf relieves the pain of bee sting.

Sage takes the sting out of insect bites.

Lemon juice (outward applications) will allay the irritation caused by the bites of gnats or flies.

Measles: Cure by eating a well roasted mouse.

Tea made from sheep pellets was used to break out measles.

Minor Burns and Scalds: Potato slices were applied to reduce the feeling of heat.

A generous application of butter, lard, or olive oil soothes the skin by keeping the air out.

Nasal Congestion: Inhale vapor from boiling vinegar and water.

Chew honeycomb as gum.

Mix 1 cup honey and ¼ cup lemon juice. Sip 1 teaspoon as needed for cough.

Neuralgia: A bag of hot sand relieves the pain of neuralgia.

> It was said that Ed Schefflin, founder of Tombstone, wore his hair long because he had suffered from neuralgia since his early teens.

Snake Bite: Apply whiskey on and in the bite, or use warm horse manure to draw out the poison.

One-half freshly killed chicken pressed against fang marks will draw out the poison — eat the other half.

Make a poultice of diced onion and strong tobacco mixed well with two tablespoons of table salt. Apply to wound and replace every six hours.

Sore Eyes: Dab eyelids with whiskey, then wipe with tip of a black cat's tail.

Sore Throat: Warm tomatoes wrapped in a rag and tied around the throat will relieve soreness.

When Marie Peters Wells of Casa Grande was a little girl, her father's favorite remedy for a sore throat or to break up a cold was to beat an egg yolk with 2 teaspoons of sugar until light and creamy, pour in a generous slug of whiskey, and then fill the glass with boiling water. Bundle up in bed and drink this concoction while hot, then quickly slide under the covers.

Spring Tonic: Sassafras tea is a good "Spring Tonic."

1 teaspoon Sassafras root to 1 cup water. Boil 10 minutes, serve hot and sweet to taste. (Root bark can be used two or three times.)

Toothache: Apply clove or cinnamon oil.

Carry a pig's tooth in your pocket and drink rye whiskey.

Take a newspaper and put it on a plate, stick a match to it, let it burn, and then blow off the paper. There will be a brownish substance left on the plate. Take a piece of cotton, wipe up this substance till the cotton is covered with it, and place this in the hollow of the tooth. Immediate relief will follow. This cure can be used also in ear ache.

Urinary and Bowel Blockage: Dandelion tea or watermelon seed tea was used. Also good for water retention.

Sweet-Sour Refresher for water retention in females.

½ cup honey
1 cup cider vinegar

Stir well and keep covered — mix 4 tablespoons with glass water.

Chill. (Drinks were cooled by lowering container tied to rope into the well or burying it in the sand.)

Whooping Cough: Drink mare's milk mixed with whiskey.

The Good of a Lemon: The juice of a lemon in hot water on awakening in the morning is an excellent liver corrective, and for stout women is better than any anti-fat medicine ever invented.

A teaspoonful of the juice of a lemon in a small cup of black coffee almost certainly relieves a bilious headache.

The Good of Tobacco: Apply tobacco poultice to wounds to stop bleeding, or use spider webs to help clotting.

Tobacco chewing helps unhealthy children grow.

Chewing tobacco is excellent for corpulent persons in that its use makes them "split their fat away."

Boil tobacco down to an extract, mix in a quantity of white pine pitch and apply to soft corns weekly until gone.

From the scrapbook of Nellie von Gerichten Smith come these suggestions on how *To Live a Century.*

It is said by observing the following rules one stands a good chance of being a worthy member of the Hundred-Year Club:

Have a room to yourself when possible, and at any rate have your own bed.

Go to bed early, and sleep at least eight hours on your right side.

Keep your bedroom window open all night.

Have a mat to your bedroom door.

Do not have your bedstead against the wall.

No cold water in the morning, but a bath at the temperature of the body.

Exercise before breakfast.

Eat a little meat, and see that it is well cooked.

Eat plenty of fat to feed the cells which destroy disease germs.

Avoid intoxicants, which destroy those cells.

Daily exercise in open air.

Allow no pet animals in your living rooms; they are likely to carry about disease germs.

Live in the country if you can.

Watch the three D's-drinking water, damp, drains.

Take frequent and short holidays.

Limit your ambition.

Doctor John Bryan McNally — a native of County Carlow, Ireland — came to Prescott to practice medicine in 1896. In June 1899 this residence located at 144 N. Grove was built by Dr. McNally, shown far right with his wife Annie, and their children: Genevieve, Margaret, John, and Joseph. The McNally home stood until the late 1970s when it was replaced by Memory Chapel. Descendants of John and Annie Sweeney McNally still live in Prescott. Photograph courtesy of Sharlot Hall Museum

Great-Aunt Genevieve McNally's Irish Coffee

Into a large whiskey goblet which has been warmed by running hot water over it, pour in one jigger (one ounce) of Irish Whiskey. Add brown sugar to taste and stir until dissolved. Then fill with warm, strong, black coffee to three-fourths full. Gently slide whipped cream on to the surface of the drink being careful not to stir the cream into the coffee and whiskey.

—McNally family

"Washing Calicoes and Muslins. — *The first requisite is plenty of water; this is even more essential for colored than for white clothes. It should not be hot enough to scald, and should have moderate suds of hard soap before the garments are put in. Very white and nice soft soap is preferable to hard for flannels — does not shrink them as much; but the latter is best for cotton goods. Wash calicoes in two waters, using but little soap in the second. When clean, rinse them two or even three times in tepid water. Good laundresses always assert that the great secret of clear muslin is thorough rinsing. The quality of starch used also affects light colors, and for muslin dresses especially only starch of the purest quality should be used. When no great stiffness is required, it is a good plan to stir the starch into the rinsing water; it assists in setting the colors where they show a tendency to run. For setting the colors of fading goods I have used ox-gall, alum, borax and salt — all with good results, though they will not 'clinch' green and blues, that are determined on taking 'French leave.' One benefit in using a strong solution of alum water is that it will make cotton fire-proof. Mothers who 'sit on thorns' at school concerts and exhibitions, watching the dangerous proximity of gossamer dresses to the foot-lights, will appreciate this advantage. And so far from injuring the looks of the muslin, there is no other treatment that will so brighten and improve the colors. Colored clothes should be wrung very thoroughly, dried in the shade, and turned about two or three times while drying." From the scrapbook of Nellie von Gerichten Smith. Photograph from the Myrtle Stephens Collection, courtesy of John Hays*

Household Hints

Women in the West were not just expected to cook, clean house, raise the children, and be a charming hostess at social gatherings. While the Arizona territory offered a wider opportunity to express oneself, often the avenues available included protecting the house and children from marauding Indians; plowing and planting crops; shucking corn; canning and preserving food; making soap and candles; sewing, washing, ironing, and mending clothes for the whole family; knitting hats, stockings, gloves, and mufflers; tending vegetable, flower, and herb gardens; delivering babies, curing cows, horses, and other livestock, and setting broken bones; giving the children at least a rudimentary education; and doing it all in a wild land where lack of supplies was much easier to deal with than loneliness.

Sometimes women could not adjust to such physical, emotional, and spiritual deprivation. San Francisco was a favorite place to wait out a husband's tour of military duty or temporary gold fever. For those who could not afford such a luxury, Arizona could seem to be a life sentence with death the only way out. But others adapted. Some, like Mollie Sawyer, who owned a saloon, gambling hall, and several rich gold mines, gave up any semblance of femininity, especially when calling for a shot glass of whiskey and her favorite cheroot. Others competed with men as business owners, hunters, gamblers, stage robbers, prospectors, and Indian fighters.

By far, the majority of women who came to the territory either with husbands or to find one, did not return to the civilization of the "States," nor did they abandon their femininity by affecting depraved attire or actions. Instead, they saw their obligation to heart and hearth as a challenge to be met. Through the unwelcome steam of a cauldron of boiling clothes, or the shimmering heat of a crock of winter preserves on an open fire, or even, at times, while resting a rifle barrel on the window sill of their cabin, they made plans for the future.

Adeline Hall (shown here in 1907) was the mother of Sharlot M. Hall. Adeline was equally well known for her medical skills and her fruit pies. Often women earned "pin money" through midwifery; selling pies, breads, preserves, herbs, vegetables, or eggs; or performing services, such as quilting bed covers or sewing a special dress.

Marie Peters Wells of Casa Grande remembers: "As my mother ran her milk route, she also got orders for piccalilli her friends made and then delivered it, too. My father had roasting ears; these, too, she sold. The hens also provided eggs for sale and it was in these ways that women made a little money."

Whenever the pioneer housewife purchased flour in one hundred pound sacks, she not only had the basic ingredient for dozens of meals, but an invaluable household aid as well. The flour sacks — once emptied and bleached — were soft, absorbent, and lint-free. They made wonderful kitchen towels and polishing cloths for dishes, silverware, windows, and furniture. They could be used as aprons and baby diapers, and they were sewn together to make curtains, sheets, and pillow cases.

There were literally hundreds of uses that flour sacks could be put to, but as a fashion accessory they were a dismal failure. One young lady in Mayer, Arizona had sewn herself a pair of panties out of the cotton sacking, and although the material was soft and her seams were fine, she had neglected to totally eradicate the flour mill's trade mark. As she bent over someone's picnic basket, a gust of wind caught up her skirt and flipped it over her head. Across her derriere it read: "Pride of the West."

Information provided by Joyce Segner (chairman of the "Big Bug Stomp," celebrating Mayer, Arizona's one hundredth anniversary) from an unpublished narrative compiled by Ione Johansen.

"*Uses for Old Bread.* — In many households a great deal of old bread goes daily into the swill pail or garbage can. Not one bit of it ought to find its way there, no matter how large or small the family. The economical housekeeper puts it all in the warming oven, and when it is thoroughly dry, grinds or rolls it and stores it away in tin cans for use. It is one of the best emergency reliances known. If company drops in suddenly to dinner, and no dessert has been prepared, it is ready to make into a bread pudding that can be baking while the family is eating the first and second courses. Served with whipped cream or fruit sauce it is delicious. A cupful of the crumbs, with two eggs and a pint of milk, will make enough to serve four people.

If one is short for potatoes in hash, a cupful will take their place, and no one will be the wiser. Added to fried potatoes, one not only gets more in quantity, but a change as well, that is very pleasing. When at your wits' end for something for tea, when the larder seems to be empty, try mixing some milk into the crumbs and fry as you would potatoes. Again, fill a cup one-third full of

95

crumbs, then cover with milk and let them stand about ten minutes. Then add the yolks of three eggs well beaten, and then the whites. Season with pepper and salt, and when ready, put a small frying pan on the stove, in which a tablespoon of butter has been heated hot. Now turn the contents of your bowl into the frying pan, let it stand a few moments on the stove where it is hot, then remove to the back of the stove, cover and let it stand about ten minutes, and then slip carefully on a hot plate and serve. This will make enough to serve four people.

For making scalloped oysters or tomatoes, bread is much nicer than crackers; also for croquettes of all kinds, the bread crumbs are more delicate than cracker crumbs or cornmeal. Eaten with milk, they are as nice as the many cereals on the market.''

—From the scrapbook of
Nellie von Gerichten Smith

Grease baking tins with beeswax, which never becomes rancid and makes unnecessary the washing of tins after each baking.

Grease the top third of a pan used for cooking any kind of pasta. When the water comes to a boil, the contents will not rise above the greased area and boil over. A tablespoon of oil in the water will keep the pasta from sticking together.

To find a honey tree, put out a saucer of sweetened water. When a bee flies to it, carefully sprinkle him with flour. Then follow the flour that falls off as he makes a ''bee line'' for the tree.

Rolls which have become dry may be freshened by dipping them quickly into water and placing them in the oven for two or three minutes until the water has dried. They will taste almost like new rolls.

To make a cup of coffee almost as nourishing as a meal, stir into it an egg well beaten. First beat the egg in a cup, add a little cream, then the sugar, and lastly the coffee, poured in gradually. Then, adding the coffee, beat constantly with a small egg-beater.

Milk which is turned or changed may be sweetened and rendered fit for use again by stirring in a little baking soda.

Salt will curdle new milk; hence, in preparing milk porridge, gravies, etc. the salt should not be added until the dish is prepared.

Fresh meat, after beginning to sour, will sweeten if placed out-of-doors in the cool, overnight.

Salt on the fingers when cleaning meat, fowls, and fish will prevent the hands from slipping.

Fish may be scaled much easier by dipping into boiling water about a minute.

Few people know that in smothering steak with onions, the flavor is greatly improved by squeezing the juice of a lemon over it.

To keep juice from soaking into pie crust, brush it with white of egg.

Canned fruit keeps its flavor and color better if each jar is wrapped in paper and kept in a cool, dark, and dry place.

If it grows underground covered in cold earth (root vegetable), then start it in cold water and cover the pot with a lid while it is cooking. If it grows above ground in the hot sun (green vegetables), then start it in hot water and leave the pot uncovered. In other words, cook vegetables in the same way as they grow and you'll never go wrong.

There is an old tip about peeling onions under water. But you cannot grate or chop onions in that way. Instead, place a slice of bread between your teeth with your mouth slightly open and breathe through your mouth. No tears will ever come to your eyes.

If you make a soup or stew too salty, drop in several raw potatoes and boil about fifteen minutes. The potatoes will not absorb the liquid but will extract some of the salt. When the dish is right, remove the potatoes and use them for frying.

Use about half a teaspoonful of baking soda in the water you boil dried beans in, and they won't "repeat" on you. This eliminates the gas that causes digestive upsets after eating beans.

If an egg is cracked, wrap it in waxed paper and twist both ends shut gently. Then boil it with the paper on.

Put a bay leaf in containers of oatmeal, cornmeal, and other dry mixes to weevils out. The taste of the leaf will not affect the meal.

Soak bacon in cold water for a few minutes to minimize the tendency to curl and shrink.

Soak potatoes in salt water for twenty minutes, and they will bake faster.

Dip a new broom in hot water before using it. This toughens the bristles and it will last longer.

To determine the freshness of an egg, place it in a glass of cold water so that it is completely submerged. If it is fresh, it will lay on its side; if it lays at an angle, it is at least three days old; and if it stands on end, it is at least ten days old.

When cooking cabbage, adding ½ cup of vinegar to the water it is cooked in will absorb all odor.

Eggshells burned to a dark brown in the oven and crushed quite fine will keep all kinds of bugs away when sprinkled on pantry shelves.

Lemon peel (and also orange) should all be saved and dried. It is a capital substitute for kindling wood. A handful will revive a dying fire and at the same time delicately perfume a room.

Store candles in a cold place — they will burn longer. Save candle stubs to coax along a fire.

Lamp wicks can be prevented from smoking by soaking them in vinegar and drying thoroughly.

Don't put wet boots and shoes by the fire to dry; instead, stuff them with newspaper. Kerosene, castor oil or warm tallow rubbed into the leather will make them pliable again and somewhat water resistant.

Kerosene will make tin tea kettles as bright as new. Saturate a woolen rag and rub with it. It will also remove stains from clean varnished furniture.

Instead of greasing your griddle, rub it with the cut side of a white turnip. There will be no taste and the griddle will not smoke.

Coal oil poured over skunk aroma on clothing will kill the smell.

Fill a dishpan half full with hot water — add half a cup sweet milk. This will soften hard water and give the greasiest dishes a bright, clean look without leaving scum; keeps hands from roughening.

Scorched fireproof dishes that have become brown from baking may have the stains removed by soaking in strong borax and water. Gently boil a partially cracked dish in sweet milk for forty-five minutes and it will be good as new.

Remove egg tarnish from silverware with moist table salt.

Half a lemon dipped in salt and rubbed on discolored ivory knife handles will restore them to their original whiteness. After doing this, wash the knives once in hot water.

Unused silver will keep bright if laid away in a box of flour.

To clean and freshen oil cloth, rub with a milk-soaked cloth, wrung out.

Mildew stains are easily removed by rubbing with a soft cloth moistened with buttermilk.

Ounce Measures

1 ounce butter equals 1 rounded tablespoon.
1 ounce flour equals 2 rounded tablespoons.
1 ounce cornstarch equals 3 level tablespoons.
1 ounce granulated sugar equals 1 rounded tablespoon.
1 ounce powdered sugar equals 2 rounded tablespoons.
1 ounce ground coffee equals 2 level tablespoons.
1 ounce grated chocolate equals 3 tablespoons.
1 ounce pepper equals 4 tablespoons.
1 ounce salt equals 2 tablespoons.
1 ounce cassia equals 4½ tablespoons.
1 ounce mustard equals 8 teaspoons.
1 ounce baking soda equal 4 teaspoons.
1 ounce baking powder equals 4 teaspoons.
1 ounce tea equals 12 teaspoons.
1 ounce nutmeg equals 5 teaspoons.
1 ounce spice equals 2 tablespoons.
1 ounce grated cheese equals ¼ cup.
1 ounce granulated gelatin equals 2 rounded tablespoons.
1 ounce equals 2 tablespoons (liquid) or 16 drachms.
1 ounce cream tartar equals 8 teaspoons.

Mary Alexander Clough was born in 1852 and came to Prescott when she was only twelve years of age. Her father, Thomas Alexander, was able to find an emigrant train of almost a dozen other families for the Alexanders to join, and it was his intention to relocate on the Russian River in California. Because the northern route was unsafe due to frequent Indian raids, the wagons were forced to follow the southern route. The group left Santa Fe, New Mexico, to cross the newly-formed territory of Arizona — marked "uncharted" on their maps — and in October 1864 arrived in the territorial capital, then consisting of a governor's "mansion" made of logs and fourteen cabins.

The members of the wagon train decided to stay in Prescott, and Mary Alexander, along with her family, participated in the first Christmas celebrated here. Thomas Alexander's decision to settle in Yavapai County proved to be an auspicious one. He was a co-discoverer of the rich Peck mine, and the town of Alexandra was named in his honor.

On April 13, 1874 Mary became Mrs. Alfred S. Clough, and she and her husband operated one of the county's first apple orchards. From Point of Rocks Ranch they shipped some of the finest fruit ever sold in the territory. Mrs. Clough is shown here in a quieter moment as she sews by the light of her living room window. Photograph courtesy of Sharlot Hall Museum

If a patch must be applied to wall paper, let the new piece lie in strong sunlight until the colors are faded to match those on the wall; then tear the edges and the applied piece will not be so conspicuous.

If you wish to make a walking skirt just to clear the ground, measure the person from the waist to the ground and deduct one and a half inches.

Home dressmakers who have difficulty in pressing curved seams will find a rolling pin a very good pressing board if a cloth is wrapped around it.

Beeswax and salt will make your rusty flatirons as clean and smooth as glass. Tie a lump of wax in a rag, and keep it for that purpose. When the irons are hot, rub them first with the wax rag, then scour with a paper or cloth sprinkled with salt.

Starch made with soapy water prevents the irons from sticking and gives a better gloss to the linen.

Use inexpensive cornstarch to keep baby and other family members dry and comfortable. Used around the neck, it will also make soiled collars easier to wash clean.

Lemon juice and salt will remove rust stains from linen without injury to the fabric. Wet the stains with the mixture and put the article in the sun. Two or three applications may be necessary if the stain is of long standing, but the remedy never fails.

Ripe tomatoes will remove ink and other stains from white cloth, also from the hands.

To whiten laces, wash them in sour milk.

Clear boiling water will remove tea stains and many fruit stains. Pour the water through the stain, and thus prevent its spreading over the fabric.

Cool rain water and soda will remove machine grease from washable fabrics.

A Simple Soap Recipe

"I never make soap by the recipe on lye cans. This is my recipe, which has never failed me: Take 4½ to 5 pounds clear, clean, salt-free meat grease (not bacon), 1 (½ pint) can lye, and 1 quart cold water. Have the grease warm (I use an old tin dishpan). Melt the lye in the water, in another vessel, and be very careful none of the lye or lye solution gets on your hands, or spatters. Now pour the melted lye in the warm grease in the dishpan and stir well for 5 minutes or more, or until both are thoroughly mixed. You will notice it getting thick. Pour the mixture in a pan (I use an old leaky meat pan, lined with clean wrapping paper). Before the soap is quite hard, cut it in squares, or pieces of any convenient size, without, however, removing from the pan. This soap is pure and white and floats. It is excellent for laundry use.

"I cannot understand why people ever boil soap — it is not at all necessary, and I call it sheer waste of time. It only takes me about 10 minutes to make soap. I always save every scrap of fat that I don't need for cooking, try it out [melt it], and strain it into my 'soap fat kettle.' Some women save pieces of fat, without trying it out, until they get enough together, but I think that is a poor way to do — the fat then smells badly, and it makes more work, than if the pieces were tried out day by day, so that a nice kettle of clean fat is ready when soap making time comes."

—From the scrapbook of
Nellie von Gerichten Smith

Note: Never make soap in an aluminum pan. Store bars of soap unwrapped; this draws moisture out and the soap lasts longer.

The early settlers of the Arizona Territory expected hardships and were prepared for them. They fought Indians, disease, starvation, and death, but the most difficult hardship they faced was the loneliness and lack of communication with another human being for weeks and often months at a time. Newspapers met an important need and were among the first businesses established in a frontier community. The Arizona Miner, whose initial edition was printed at Fort Whipple on March 9, 1864, was one of the earliest newspapers in the territory. It proudly proclaimed itself "The Official Paper of Arizona" and took its duties very seriously, publishing mining laws and minutes of the territorial legislature in full, all official proclamations from the governor's office, reports — down to the slightest detail of dress and drink — of all receptions for dignitaries, community balls and socials, private and public dinners, and theatrical productions. Under a column entitled "Local Intelligence" was listed the latest gossip — from Indian rumors to who came and went on the weekly stage. A clipping from the 1880s scrapbook of Nellie von Gerichten Smith, wife of Barney Smith who owned the Palace Saloon, noted that "a newspaper is a window through which men look out on all that is going on in the world; without a newspaper a man is shut in a small room and knows little or nothing of what is happening outside of himself. In our day the newspapers keep pace with history and record it."

John Marion, probably the Miner's most flamboyant editor-owner, filled its columns with a delightful mixture of news and nostalgia for the old days.

The "Betterments"

For men, Arizona was an exciting adventure. Here one could forget lost loves, lost causes, past transgressions, former wives, and creditors. The frontier beckoned with its promise of riches, unlimited land, and the freedom to enjoy life to the fullest. Here, Indian attacks, the harsh terrain, and the violence, ignorance, and cupidity of one's companions spurred men on to gallant deeds or petty meanness — and an alias could always be arranged whenever circumstances dictated. Here beans, bacon, and biscuits were fine enough fare and a tent or shack served nicely as a gin mill, gambling hall, bordello, and boarding house — often all at the same time.

Sharlot Hall, who arrived in Prescott with her family in February 1882, knew from observing the life lead by her mother and other early settlers that "the old frontier was a man's life — not a woman's; and the men who flocked to it were not domestic; they were adventurers at heart — drawn by the boundless freedom, the chance for sudden and easy gain, the lack of restraint and respectability, and the picturesque wildness of the life. They were not homemakers in any deep sense; the handles of the plow did not fit readily in their hands; it was easier to look for gold in the hills than to plant corn in the valleys. They were of that type where the big end of the family log falls naturally to the woman; in the beauty and wildness and varied opportunity of this new land they did not miss the comforts and refinements of living for which the women constantly struggled. So it fell to the women to bear on their hearts the weight of the homes that were yet to be, and to temper the great conquest of a

"I was here," he crowed, "when two men right across Granite Creek were killed by Indians, and when it took a lady's stocking full of gold just to buy a sack of flour. . . . They tried to get my scalp, both the Indians and white men, but damn 'em, I'm still here!"

Marion also editorially called for improvements he felt were needed in the community. In the January 10, 1879 Miner he reported: "Edison has at last got down to a rough estimate of the cost of making electric light. He can make 600 lights for twelve hours for $6.50 whereas gas in New York costs $51.00. Let's have electric lights in Prescott." Subsequently Marion announced: "Electric lights will illuminate the town this p.m. What a change from camp fires and rascally candles! We would get letters and papers six weeks old and read them by campfire while the Indians shot arrows at us."

Through the pages of the Arizona Miner and later the Prescott Morning Courier, John Marion used his influence to advocate public schooling for area children, a telegraph line, free public library, a public water-works, good hotel accommodations for Prescott, a railroad linking areas of agricultural and mining importance throughout Central Arizona, range conservation, a theater and other cultural advancements, and recognition for the pioneer settlers of the territory. Photograph courtesy of Sharlot Hall Museum

wild land with the best that civilization has to bring. The mutual need bred a spirit of mutual helpfulness and these women by their own labor brought comfort out of the barest and roughest surroundings, [and] also kept alive the social instincts, the desire for culture and improvement, for education and all that is best in civilization.''

From the ''hurdy-gurdy'' girls, who encouraged bathing and shaving among the slovenly miners and cowboys by ignoring those who didn't, to the influential members of the literary, library, and drama societies, women felt a significant responsibility to exhibit cultural and moral standards and urge their acceptance in the community. The ''betterments'' which the ladies insisted upon included fine homes, majestic churches, the most modern libraries and schools, as well as social and cultural organizations and events to rival anything available ''back in the States.''

In the spring of 1871 Reverend Alexander Gilmore, the first Army chaplain stationed at Fort Whipple, began instructing the youth of Prescott. The Miner of June 3 reported that "the sum of $308.00 has been subscribed toward the supporting of the school now being taught by Chaplain Gilmore, and as a school census will soon be taken and taxes collected, the chances are pretty good that a school will, hereafter, be kept running pretty steadily." The first term closed on August 18, 1871, and one of Gilmore's students, fourteen-year-old Josephine Stephens wrote: "We are requested by our teacher to prepare a composition to be read upon this our last day of school. I am truly sorry that our school must close and think it truly shameful that the large city of Prescott cannot or will not support a school for more than three months at a time. Just as we are getting started in our studies the school funds give out and the school closes. Then perhaps in the course of six months or a year someone takes up another subscription and the school starts again and having forgotten nearly all that we learned the term before back we go again and the expiration of each term finds us in the same place. How can our parents and friends expect us to acquire an education under such circumstances? We hope all who have come today to witness our examinations will see the necessity of a continuous school and will go forth resolved to do all in there (sic) power to that end and it is with deep regret that I bid my schoolmates goodby and shall always look back with pleasure to the many happy days we have passed together hoping however that after a short vacation we may again assemble and resume our studies."

In some very fortunate communities, "schoolin' " had a sponsor. Mayer, Arizona had such good fortune in the person of its founder, Joseph Mayer. He not only built the first school house and provided a wagon to pick the children up and return them home, but paid the teacher's first month's salary. He and his wife, Sarah Belle, affectionately called "Sadie," provided room and board in their home for the

105

teacher and several students who lived too far from school to go home every afternoon. Shown in this photograph of the Big Bug school at Mayer which was taken in 1891 or 1892 are (front row — seated) Harry McMichael and the Taylor children, (front row — standing) Maggie and Dick Hildebrandt and Joseph Mayer's son, Wilbur Joseph called "Bur" by everyone, (back row — left to right) Dottie Long, Melissa Lane, Jennie McCarthy, Jessie Lane, Carri McCarthy, Kate Scarlet, Lena Hartsfield, Mary Bell "Mamie" Mayer, Ed Hartsfield, and Jack McCarthy. Standing in the doorway is the teacher, Mr. A. E. Joscelyn.

Education was regarded by the pioneer populace as a necessary tool towards improving the lives of their children. Even the most remote cattle ranch or mining claim tried to provide instruction in reading and writing through the use of the family Bible. But sometimes even that was not available.

Lois Boblett, who arrived in the territory with her husband in 1864 wrote: "There were no school or church in Arizona when we went there, and none for several years later. When we became responsible for Charles and Bell [Isabel] I was very anxious for them to have a better chance then I ever had so I was determined that they would and wondered how I could manage as I had to leave all of my old school books on the Reaverday where we lost all our cattle and we took no papers and I tho't of some little pie plates we had. They were tin and had the alphabet stamped on them so I taught them their letters on these plates, then they started a Sunday School in Prescott and they would send me papers and I taught them to read and spell out of those papers." Photographs courtesy of Sharlot Hall Museum

One of the most important resolutions passed by the First Territorial Legislature when it met in Prescott during September and October of 1864 was to appropriate the sum of two hundred fifty dollars for the establishment of schools in Prescott, La Paz, Mojave, and Tucson — with the provision that each settlement must raise matching funds for either private or public education. Books consisted of whatever publications had been packed in trunks and covered wagons; pencils or chalks were broken in two and shared to make them go further. When there was a shortage of these supplies, the students used charcoal to mark words and numbers on flat wooden paddles. If a private home was not available, then school was usually conducted in an unused building with plank benches for the students; desks and stoves were luxuries found only as physical facilities improved throughout the settlement. Education was available through subscription only, usually a few dollars a week in advance.

Excerpts from the Diary of Sister Monica 1870

"After bidding adieu to our good Sisters in Carondelet, we started on our long and perilous journey to Arizona. Our first two stations were St. Joseph's and St. Bridget's Asylums, St. Louis, Mo., where we were cordially greeted by our good Sisters. We then wished them goodbye, and repaired to the Pacific Railway Depot, took the car at 6:00 p.m. direct to Kansas City. Puff! Puff! went the locomotive and we were off, really, indeed on our way to Arizona.

"It is quite probable we may never meet here below; and it is only when this thought occurs to me, that I know how deeply I love them. How consoling to know with an infallible certainty that we are accomplishing the will of God, with an assured hope of being reunited in our Heavenly Country, to those beloved ones we have left here below, for the love of Jesus and the salvation of souls.

"**April 21, 1870** — We changed cars during the night — it was, indeed, a change in every respect as the cars were filled with emigrants, crying children, etc. To conclude from the offensive atmosphere in the cars, they must have had any amount of spoiled chicken, eggs, cigars, etc. In this motly crowd we spent the remainder of our second night.

"**April 22, 1870** — In the morning we refreshed ourselves with a nice cup of coffee, then proceeded on our journey. The weather was cool and pleasant — an Indian boy played the violin for the entertainment of the passengers. Reverend Mother treated us to apples and maple sugar. As we approached Omaha, some of us were crying, some praying, but all were looking eagerly to see if the train was there. We did not wait long, as a passenger came with the welcome news that the train had just left. Thanks be to God! escaped from every lip, and was in every heart.

"**April 25, 1870** — At five o'clock, we passed the "Thousand Mile Tree," so called from its being just a thousand miles from Omaha. It stands at the entrance of the Devil's Gate, a very appropriately named place, with lofty mountains rising on each side of the track."

On April 27, a week after leaving their convent, the Sisters arrived in San Francisco. After a three day rest, they "took passage on the steamer 'Arizola'" to San Diego.

"**May 7, 1870** — We left in a private conveyance for Fort Yuma. The carriage was too small for all to ride inside, consequently one was obliged to ride outside with the driver. Sister Ambrosia volunteered to make the great sacrifice, the act of mortification and humility. It is beyond description what she suffered in riding two hundred miles in a country like this without protection from the rays of the tropical sun.

"At noon we halted and took lunch in a stable twelve miles from San Diego. Sr. Maximum and I went in search of gold; seeing quantities of it, we proposed getting a sack and filling it. Just think! a sack of gold! but we soon learned from experience that 'all is not gold that glitters.' We camped about sunset, at the foot of a mountain, made some tea and took our supper off a rock. We wished Reverend Mother could see us at supper.

"After offering thanks to the Giver of all good, we retired to rest — Mother, Sr. Euphrasia and Sr. Martha under the wagon, others inside where there was room for two to lie down. Sr. Euphrasia and I sat in a corner and tried to sleep. We had scarcely closed our eyes when the wolves began to howl about us. We were terribly frightened and recommended ourselves to the safe-keeping of Him who guides the weary traveller on his way. We feared they would consume our little store of provisions and let us perish in the wilderness; but the driver told us not to fear. During the night, Sr. Euphrasia was startled from her sleep by one of the horses licking her face. She screamed fearfully and we concluded she was a prey to the wolves.

"**May 8, 1870** — Feast of the Patronage of our Holy Father, St. Joseph, we were determined to celebrate it the best way we could. After offering up our prayers, we formed a procession, going in advance of the wagon — Mother walking in front, bearing a Spanish lily in her hand. We followed in solemn order and imagined ourselves in Egypt.

"At noon, we came to a cool shady place, in which we rested. The ranchman (a person who keeps refreshments, stable feed, etc., on the western plains) invited us to dinner. He offered us a good meal of all we could desire. There were several ranchmen there from the neighboring stations, but no women. There are few women in this country. After dinner they became very sociable. We retired to the stable where our driver and only protector was, and they followed. Some of them proposed marriage to us, saying we would do better by accepting the offer than by going to Tucson, for we would all be massacred by the Indians. The simplicity and earnestness with which they spoke put indignation out of the question, as it was evident they meant no insult, but our good. They were all native Americans. For that afternoon, we had amusement enough. We then resumed our journey.

"That evening we camped in a very damp place, made some tea, the only beverage we had. The night was very cold. I think there was a frost. We had only one blanket between seven of us. Sr. Martha and I had only light summer shawls; the others were fortunate enough to have brought their winter ones along.

"We were much fatigued, and though hard the bed and cold the night, we soon fell asleep. Between two and three in the morning, we were startled by an unearthly yell from Sr. Martha and one from the driver. We hastened to learn the matter. The Sisters in the wagon, feeling cold, concluded to kindle a fire to warm themselves. Sr. Martha thought she saw a fine large stick among the dry leaves, and eagerly grabbed it; when the leaves fell off, she perceived it was the leg of a man. She then yelled, and he screamed, but only for mischief. It was the driver who was resting himself among the dry leaves. It was well that they did wake up for we were almost stiff with the cold. After warming ourselves a little, we made some tea to refesh ourselves.

"**May 9, 1870** — We spent the day in climbing up and down hills. In the evening we reached the ever memorable place, 'Mountain Springs,' the entrance of the American desert. For several miles the road is up and down mountains. We were obliged to travel it on foot; at the highest point it is said to be 4,000 feet above sea level. We were compelled to stop here to breathe. Some of the Sisters lay down on the roadside, being unable to proceed further. Beside this terrible fatigue we suffered still more from thirst. After a few moments rest, we began to descend. We were so much fatigued that it seemed as if our limbs were dislocated. We had yet two miles to descend on foot, the greater part being very steep.

"The sides of the road were covered with teams of horses, oxen and cattle which had dropped dead trying to ascend. When Mother beheld so many dead animals she wept, fearing we might share the same fate.

"We travelled as fast as we were able in order to reach the ranch for we were almost dead with thirst. We expected nothing but a drink of water and we were not disappointed. After refreshing ourselves with a drink of cold water, we retired to the stable yard.

"There were upwards of twenty men there, some of whom were intoxicated. They annoyed us very much; some offered to shake hands with us, others trying to keep them off, and all swearing, etc. We will never be able to tell our dear Sisters all the mortifications and humiliations we had to endure there. It was nine o'clock before we could get a chance to make some tea; in the meantime we remained near our carriage — it was our only home.

"Four of us slept in a shanty; the cook brought us a blanket, and after picking some 'grey backs' off of it, presented it to us. The men were coming in and going out all night. We asked the cook what it all meant. He replied in a somewhat embarrassed manner that 'ladies seldom pass this way, and when they do the men wish to enjoy their society.'

"**May 10, 1870** — We started this morning at five o'clock and entered the desert. It is a vast bed of sand. Travelling over it is rendered dangerous on account of the sand storms. We were told they found a government wagon, loaded with fire arms, which had been forwarded several months before, and a stage coach with seven passengers, all buried in the sand.
"In one place, we passed a drove of horned cattle, said to contain a thousand head; everyone died of heat that same day. Another place we passed the remains of 1,500 sheep, smothered in a sand storm. We could get water only in one place, and when we did get it, it was not only hot, but so full of minerals that we suffered more after taking it than before.

"**May 12, 1870** — Although nearly overcome with fatigue, everyone was

109

full of courage. The man offered us the far room to sleep in at a ranch we arrived at, but we said we preferred the stable. He replied there were forty men in the stable. Six of them gave us their places and in a twinkling of an eye we were fast asleep, and did not wake until 7 a.m. We then saw the strange place we were in, forty men, sure enough, and as many Indians. Nevertheless, they all treated us with the greatest respect and kindness. The weather was extremely hot, and we were so sorely fatigued that the driver advised us to wait until evening."

At 10 a.m. on May 13, the Sisters reached Arizona City (now Yuma) where they "had the pleasure of hearing a Spanish sermon for the first time."

On May 17, the Sisters, accompanied by Father Francisco and a cook with a wagonful of provisions, left Arizona City for their final destination, Tucson. Sister Monica described "the average heat in the shade being 125 degrees," and yet at night they "suffered much from the cold."

"**May 21, 1870** — We started on our way at 4 a.m. and passed many recently made graves of persons killed by Indians. One of these contained the remains of a father, mother, and five children. These burial places looked so sadly neglected. The desolate lonely places in which these poor creatures were laid to rest, their melancholy and sad deaths, cast a damper over our spirits, as we had no certainty of not meeting the same fate. We passed at night the Indian place of worship; huge, immovable rocks on which they have cut the figures of their gods, their various planets, different animals of the forest, and even reptiles."

"**May 24, 1870** — We started early, entering upon the most dangerous portion of our journey, as we were in danger of being attacked and massacred by Indians at any moment. About 4 p.m. we passed through the valley of the Pima Indians. Their costume consists of two pieces of calico or flannel, extending to the knees, one piece hanging in front and the other behind. The young squaws are clothed with the inner bark of the trees, the old ladies are not so modestly attired. They dress their hair in a mixture of mud and water, which has the double effect of destroying the vermin and keeping the hair in place.

"**May 25, 1870** — Whilst at breakfast in the morning, three of the citizens of Tucson rode up. Some miners joined us in order to share our protection. Soldiers followed close in the rear. At noon we reached the station where the remainder of the escort from Tucson was awaiting — 65 miles from the city. There was great rejoicing among them, but as they could not speak either French or English, we did not understand them. We set out again, everyone in fine spirits. All passed off pleasantly until midnight, when a serious turn of mind and manner seemed to take possession of everyone. We were then approaching Picacho Peak, where the Apaches were accustomed to attack travellers. A fearful massacre had been perpetrated only a week previous. The place is literally filled with graves. Each one prepared his firearms, even good Father Francisco. The citizens pressed around our carriage. The soldiers road (sic) about like blood hounds. In passing through the peak, the horses began to neigh, a sure indication of the close proximity of the savages. 'The Indians!' was echoed from every mouth. Whip and spurs were given to the horses — we went like lightning — the men yelling all the time like so many fiends, in order to frighten the savages.

"May 26, 1870 — After refreshing ourselves with a cup of coffee, we continued our journey until within fifteen miles of Tucson. The citizens wished us to remain there all night, as they wished to enter Tucson in daylight, where a grand reception was in preparation. You see, they were quite proud of us! After considerable reasoning they became quite enthusiastic over the matter, but Father finally obtained their consent for us to enter that night. Four men went in advance with the joyful news of our arrival. The ladies and children had stationed themselves on the housetops, being too modest to mix in the crowd with the men. About three miles from the town, we were met by the procession, which was headed by four priests on horseback; as we came in sight they dismounted, and ran rather than walked, to meet us, the crowd in the meantime discharging firearms. Before we reached the city, their number increased to about 3,000, some discharging firearms, others bearing lighted torches, all walking in order with their heads uncovered. The city was illuminated, the fireworks in full play. Balls of combustible matter were thrown into the streets through which we passed; at every explosion, Sister Euphrasia made the sign of the cross. All the bells in the city were pealing forth their merriest strains. A nice supper had been prepared for us. When we had finished our repast, they departed, leaving us in quiet possession of our new home, 'St. Joseph's Convent, Tucson, Arizona.'"

The *Arizona Citizen* of October 4, 1879 reported that in 1870, the first year that the Sisters operated the convent, seventy-nine women of Mexican ancestry entered to receive holy instruction and eventually take their vows. Sisters from the Tucson convent went on to establish schools and hospitals throughout the territory, including those in Prescott, Phoenix, and Tombstone.

Shown in this early photograph of St. Joseph's Academy, then on Marina Street next to the newly-constructed (1895) Sacred Heart Church, is, left to right:

1st row (bottom) — Fern Robinson, Maud Murphy, Fern Duke, unidentified, Mary Farley, unidentified, Beryl Jean Jamison, unidentified, Dick Hildebrandt, Walter Murphy.

2nd row — Lawrence Massing, unidentified, unidentified, Frances Massing, unidentified, Eula Picket, Louise Hill, Malcolm Barrett, Beverly Burk.

3rd row — Lila Campbell, unidentified, Ethel Love, Mary Fitzgerald, Herman McDonald, Leona Murphy, Elsie Duke, unidentified, Blanche McDonald, Maud Hanna.

4th row — Diego Monreal, Frank Murphy, Fred McMahon, unidentified, unidentified, unidentified, unidentified, unidentified, unidentified, unidentified.

5th row — Ed Farley, Earl Nash, Fred Eckert, unidentified, unidentified, unidentified, Homer Zettler, unidentified, Katie Burton, unidentified.

6th row — unidentified, Hazel "Pet" O'Sullivan, Theresa Sidel, Sister Mary Rose, unidentified, unidentified, Marie Derr, Ellen "Pat" O'Sullivan, Mary Murphy, unidentified. Photograph courtesy of Sharlot Hall Museum

By the 1890s the Salvation Army was making spiritual inroads throughout the more populated areas of the Arizona territory. They brought religion to the boomtowns where more conservative sects might have feared to trod, daring the Devil to do battle wherever they found him. And in Arizona, they didn't have to look very far!

This contingent of the Salvation Army made their headquarters in Globe. The only members of the group who are identified are, (front row — third from left) Mrs. Jack James, a convert; (fourth and fifth from the left) Captain and Mrs. West, the group's spiritual leaders; (back row, first from the left) Fred Ealden, a member of the Army; and (second from left) Jack James, a convert, formerly known as "Tobacco Jack."

In Prescott, the fact that the Salvation Army consisted of only two rather pretty young ladies did not stop Captain Maud Bigney and her assistant, Captain Clara Clemo, from making quite an impression on "Whiskey Row." First, they rented the Road to Ruin saloon as their headquarters, and lived there rather than accepting the accommodations offered on Nob Hill. Then they held their first street meeting in front of the biggest and best known saloon/hotel along the Row — the Palace. As if that weren't enough, they entered that and a number of other establishments, urging the bartenders, brothel owners, gamblers, and prostitutes to turn away from their sinful professions. When the good citizens of Prescott realized what would happen to the local economy if the Row closed, financial support of the Salvation Army ended abruptly. Photograph courtesy of the Department of Library, Archives and Public Records, State of Arizona

Arizona was not totally filled with people who exhibited man's baser qualities. Many of the men, women, and families who came here in the early days were law-abiding and God-fearing citizens, but it was hard to stay that way for long.

Religion was bad for business. In 1887 George Barnard, the owner of Prescott's Juniper House restaurant from the spring of 1864 until it burned to the ground in March of 1865, was proprietor of a saloon in Phoenix on First Avenue, near Washington Street. When dunned for a debt, he complained that he found it difficult to pay his bills because of "a complete change of customs in this community since the advent of civilizing forces, viz; the advent of *Railroads* and *Preachers.*" An issue of the *Tombstone Prospector* told of an incident in Charleston: "One 'Parson' Brown attempted to hold divine services there sometime in 1878, when a cowboy put in an appearance and not only made the parson desist, but, with six-shooters leveled at his head, made him dance; whereupon a committee of citizens took the matter in hand, invited the Rev. Brown to preach at a certain hour, when all business was closed and people turned out en masse to hear him."

Violence was probably very high on the prayer list for those who did attend church. No doubt, protection was implored not just against the elements and Indians but also against the bad men, cattle rustlers, and shootists who roamed the territory at will. Charleston, about ten miles southwest of Tombstone near the border with Mexico, was a hide-out for many of these outlaws and while the citizens tolerated their presence — and their business — it took a parson with lots of grit to stand up to them. One Sunday, none other than William Brocius, alias William Graham, alias "Curly Bill," attended church in Charleston accompanied by his gang. He assured the rather nervous preacher that they were not there to cause trouble, whereupon the man, seizing an opportunity he might never have again, changed the text of his sermon to Matthew 26:52, "All they that take the sword shall perish with the sword." Curly Bill showed no hint of agitation and even passed the hat for the congregation, who responded with the largest collection ever made by that church, before or since. The next day, Justice of the Peace Jim Bennett fined Curly Bill twenty-five dollars for disturbing the peace. The outlaw paid and then announced that church had turned out to be by far the most expensive of his amusements.

As the territory began to feel the influences of "civilization," attending church became less hazardous, but it was still a far cry from pious meditation and stained glass windows. George Whitwell Parsons attended services in Tombstone at every opportunity and commented in his journal in March of 1880: "Plenty of loose women left the church for the saloon. Don't see their object in attending." Actually, the church was not all that far from the saloon, for he writes on Sunday, April 4, 1880: "Attended church in town this a.m. Talked with the minister a while before service. Hard work for him to preach on account of Dance House racket in rear. Calls to rally in that direction do not mingle well — 'hug gals in corner,' etc. The place is a rather poor one for divine services."

Josephine Stephens, whose father was a partner in the Kelly and Stephens mercantile house on the northwest corner of Gurley and Montezuma (where Sun United Drugs is today) noted the arrival of the first Baptist minister in town: "August 17, 1879 — The new Preacher preached by a name of Winds (sic) lots of people was at church." Reverend Adolphus Windes recalled in

114

later years: "I will never forget that first service in Prescott. There was only one hymn book, and that the one my wife and I had brought across the plains in the immigrant wagon." On January 25, 1880 the Windeses helped to establish the first Baptist church in Prescott, and later that year they also organized churches in Globe, Jerome, and the Verde. Reverend Windes "arrived in Phoenix in 1882 and found it a small town of Mexican adobes, streets deep in dust, the post office — the show place of the town — a common little shack. In those days it was difficult to find rooms for rent in any other form than a flat top adobe, all in a row. A drygoods box served as the dining room table, and smaller boxes were used as chairs."

Not only was life hard for the man who chose to follow the ministry, but the general cynicism of the citizens was very disheartening. This undated excerpt from the *Arizona Miner* gives a fairly true indication of the general sentiment on the subject: "For a town so blessed with churches and minister, Prescott can boast of possessing more 'Bible-backed,' psalm-singing, sanctimonious, hypo-critical and lying slanderers and villifiers than any town of the same size in the world. An intimate acquaintance with the majority of Prescott's 'uncogude' will convince any respectable man that if God Almighty has ever bothered himself by preparing mansions in the skies for such cantering cattle, he has wasted much valuable time."

Despite the odds, both ministers and their congregations persevered. Churches offered a solace and introduced decorum into a wild society, and the very souls they sought to save sometimes helped remind the pious that they shared a common bond. The *Miner* of February 27, 1876 reported that "during the administration of the sacrement of the Lord's Supper on Sunday evening last at the meeting on McCormick Street, notwithstanding the solemnity of the occasion, the congregation, not excepting some of the Ministers, were constrained to smile, some of them audibly, at a ludicrous event that transpired. A poor old drunken simpleton known as 'Dr. Hess,' whose breath was so charged with the fumes of whiskey as to render him a nuisance to those near him in the audience, walked up with the communicants and made a dive for the bottle containing the sacremental wine. The presiding elder, Rev. A. Groves, happened to take in the situation at a glance and 'stood him off' but he was hard to bluff, and contended for several minutes for a drink. He didn't seem to care for the bread but felt like communing with them in wine. Parson Groves tried very hard to keep a straight face, as the solemn surroundings required, and at one time essayed to weep with those who wept and were unconscious of the ridiculous scene that was being enacted, but we could discover beneath his hands, with which he attempted to cover his face, that he was in the condition of the boy who 'couldn't cry for laughing.'"

The Congregational Church was the second to organize for formal worship in Prescott and the first church of its sect to hold services in the territory. This structure was dedicated on November 27, 1881, and on December 12 and 13, 1883 was the scene of the first organizational convention of the Arizona Women's Christian Temperance Union.

Standing in front of the church is Ida Florentine Williams, who was, according to her son, H. L. Davisson, the first school teacher in Jerome. When she was two years old, Ida's family joined an emigrant train in Missouri and headed for California along the Santa Fe Trail. They arrived here on August 15, 1875, and "Grampaw" Williams got a job in J. M. Sanford's shingle camp, so they left the train and settled in Prescott. Photograph courtesy of Sharlot Hall Museum

Reverend Hiram Walter Read organized one of the first Sabbath Schools in the territory on August 7, 1864 and probably conducted it in "Fort Misery" where he also held the town's first religious services. Unfortunately, it was not well attended and was discontinued.

Then in early June 1866 another Sabbath School was organized by Harriet Miller Turner (shown here), wife of William F. Turner, first Chief Justice of Arizona; Etta Parker Bashford, wife of Coles A. Bashford, president of the First Territorial Legislature; and Mary Catherine Leib Brooks, the only woman with Governor Goodwin's party of territorial officials, as wife of the military surgeon Charles Leib. Her second husband, Hezekiah Brooks, was a judge and one of the townsite commissioners.

The Arizona Miner reported that on Christmas 1868, "several gentlemen of this town have presented Mrs. William F. Turner with a costly silk dress, as a token of their esteem for her as a lady, and as a reward for her efforts to instruct the children of Prescott in the way they should go, a work in which she has been engaged for over two years past in the Sunday School established by her." Photograph courtesy of the Department of Library, Archives and Public Records, State of Arizona

Prescott had its first brass band in 1865, and during the summer months Sunday concerts on the Plaza were an enjoyable event after church and again in the evening after supper. Members of the community bands were lured to Prescott by the good jobs offered them if they promised to play in the band. Jules Baumann, owner of Baumann's Candy and Ice Cream Factory, was one of Prescott's best known bandmasters, and "Professor" Achille La Guardia, Regimental Bandmaster for the Eleventh Infantry band at Fort Whipple, conducted a number of band concerts on the Plaza. La Guardia and his family, including son, Fiorello, (later the colorful mayor of New York City) gave musical performances, as well.

Shown in this circa 1910s photograph are: (left to right) Jim Laudenslauger, William Linden, Otis Crose, "Butch" Smith, Julius Jacoby, Dan Howser, Dick Liner, A. A. Emanuel, Ernest Emanuel, Howard Crose, George Crose, Charles Travis, and, standing in front, bandmaster Jules Baumann. The buildings seen along the skyline include (left to right) Bank of Arizona, at the corner of Cortez and Gurley; R. H. Burmister and Sons mercantile store; the Knights of Pythias building; unidentified; William Ross's Drug Store; unidentified; Prescott Home Bakery; unidentified. The roof line above the Home Bakery is that of the Episcopal church. To the left of the church, on the corner of Marina and Union, is the house built in 1899 by Ed Block. Behind the Rough Rider statue can be seen the fly wing of the Elks Opera House. The buildings to the right of the Episcopal church are the elegant homes along the

top of Union Street, which were dubbed "Nob Hill."

There were a number of other cultural and social organizations in the community, including Aztlan Lodge No. 1 of the Free and Accepted Masons, the first of that order to organize (on July 25, 1865) in the territory; the first Arizona lodge of the Independent Order of Odd Fellows, which began holding meetings here on July 13, 1868; contingents of Eastern Star, Knights Templar, Knights of Pythias, the Benevolent and Protective Order of Elks, the Ladies Literary Group, a number of theatrical societies both in town and at Fort Whipple, as well as women's fellowships connected with the various religious denominations. Of course, not all organizations professed such auspicious beginnings or lofty goals. The March 22, 1879 issue of the Arizona Miner reported that Brecht & Throne's big wagon derrick on Granite Creek had been toppled as a prank. Twenty young men were fined twenty dollars by the Justice of the Peace for malicious mischief and ordered to replace the derrick forthwith. "The raising of that derrick was a town jubilee. The young men, necessarily having to brave it out, there and then organized the 'Derrick Club.' " Photograph courtesy of Sharlot Hall Museum

Fannie Stevens gave Prescott's first music lessons using a small lap organ which she and her husband brought overland from San Francisco, California. Nellie von Gerichten, shown here, also came to Prescott from San Francisco, where she had been the first woman to play violin with the philharmonic orchestra of that city.

Barney Smith heard of Nellie's musical abilities and asked her to entertain at his place of business, the Palace Saloon. To see that Nellie's reputation was properly protected, her mother accompanied her to Prescott and sat next to Nellie during every performance. The pretty and talented miss soon won the heart of Barney Smith, and they were married. He built a house for her at 511 West Gurley and a conservatory next door where Nellie gave music lessons.

From 1878 until the 1930s she wrote musical scores as well as a number of children's stories and poems on the backs of music sheets. "Edna's Adventures In The Wonderland of Music" tells the story of Edna, aged six, and Roma, aged four, who lived in a house next to "a piano and violin teacher, and her husband. They had no children." The two "spent many hours each day at the teacher's house, whom they affectionately called Tante." (German for Grandmother.)

Nellie G. Smith encouraged her students to put on amateur shows at the Elks Opera House to accustom them to public exposure and teach them the appreciation of a live audience. She began teaching music to Prescott's children when they were quite small and never seemed to tire of instilling a love of music in them. One of her stories ends with the lines:

"Little hands can make sweet music,
If they practice every day;
Each little finger will get stronger,
Until they all know how to play.
Then what pleasure you will give
To mama dear, and papa too,
If you will only practice daily
They will be so proud of you.
Learn to love your music, children,
As you love your dolls and toys.
For what you love to do, seems easy;
So practice, little girls and boys."

Georgia Weaver (shown here, circa 1890s) was born in Prescott on July 7, 1871 to Caroline Stephens Weaver, daughter of Varney A. Stephens, and Benjamin Henry Weaver. Georgia's maternal grandparents came to the territory in 1863, and her father (see insert) first entered the area later known as Arizona in 1861 as a member of the First California Infantry, part of the Army of the Pacific. In the fall of 1862 he held the government and military mail contract for a one hundred mile radius to and from Yuma, then known as Arizona City. Ben had apprenticed at an early age as a printer and worked at that and a number of other jobs before joining Governor Goodwin's party of territorial officials in 1863 at the age of twenty-seven. Weaver became printer for the Arizona Miner, Prescott's first newspaper, and was co-owner with John H. Marion from September 1867 to February 1875.

Georgia, referred to by many as Georgie, grew up in a close family of three sisters and a brother, surrounded by an assortment of grandparents, aunts, uncles, and cousins. Her aunt, Josephine Stephens, wrote about Georgia often in the diary she kept in 1879 and 1880:

"October 1 — 1879 I commenced to give Georgie her lesson in music

"October 27 — 1879 I have commenced on Cora and Georgie dresses trimmed in blue and red plaid

"November 1 — 1879 I went with Georgie to have her tooth pulled Doc [Warren E.] Day pulled it

"November 22 — 1879 Georgie is still taking music lessons."

Georgia's older sister, Cora Weaver Johns, was also musically inclined and played the wedding march for her marriage to John Morrison Aitken on December 8, 1892. This photograph of Georgia at the piano may have been taken at her parents' residence on upper Montezuma Street or in her own home on North Granite Street. Photograph of Georgia Weaver courtesy of Dorthy J. Jones. Insert of Benjamin Weaver from the Myrtle Stephens Collection, courtesy of John Hays

Social gatherings were a very important part of life on the western frontier because in this way the pioneer populace could forget the hardships and dispel loneliness. Even for pioneers on their way to the Arizona territory, the evening gathering around the campfire was an enjoyable and highly anticipated event. Everyone was expected to participate in the entertainment with a song, or story, or perhaps by playing a fiddle, banjo, or other musical instrument brought to the wilderness by covered wagon. Soon the merriment eased tired bodies, and the weary miles trudged that day were forgotten. If a floor was lacking, a wagon cover stretched tightly on the ground made a good dancing place. Lanterns were hung in the pine trees to give light and someone stood guard with a rifle in case prowling Indians were attracted to the party. In one of Sharlot Hall's old notebooks are recorded the following "dance calls":

S'lute yer pardners! Let 'er go!
Balance all an' do-se-do.
Swing yer girl an' run away!
Right an' left an' gents sashay.
Gents to right an' swing 'er cheat!
On to the next gal an' repeat.
Balance next an' don't be shy!
Swing yer pard an' swing 'er high!
Bunch the girls an' circle round.
Whack yer feet until they sound!

Form a basket. Break away.
Swing an' kiss an' all git gay!
Al'man left an' balance all!
Lift yer hoofs an' let 'em fall.
Swing yer op'sites! Swing agin!
Kiss the sage hens if ye kin!
Back to pardners, do-se-do.
All join hands an' off ye go!
Gents, s'lute yer little sweets!
Hitch an' promenade to seats!

The first community ball was held in Prescott on November 8, 1864, and women were very scarce. Even by 1888 that situation had not improved much. Samuel M. Boblett wrote the following letter to Mr. Richard Culver on December 5: "We are going to have a little party on Friday Night December the 14th 1888 at the Murray School House at the Lynx Creek Crossing. Sure want you to come and bring your sister and all the rest of the girls you can get."

Besides being a wonderful break in the daily difficulties of life, parties were considered an important indicator of social standing. Lois Boblett noted in her journal: "The Masons used to come get me to get their lodge suppers and one time I got up a wedding supper. Another time they came to me to get a supper for a dance, one man living with a Mexican woman was not invited. He supposed we had the inviting to do and he was very angry and came to the house the next day and was going to shoot Ed, but he happened to be out. He went home and got a revolver and swore that he would kill Mr. Boblett, or Ed, as I always called my husband. That day their (sic) was a funeral and Ed attended it and as they were marching out to the grave, a friend of ours stepped up to Ed and gave him a revolver, telling him to shoot the man on sight for he was hunting for Ed to kill him. Ed kept out of his way till he got sober, then he was not on the kill quite so much."

In order to avoid disputes at dances and other social gatherings, there was often a Floor Manager whose duties included admitting only those who were considered reputable citizens and seeing that any fisticuffs were quickly brought under control. He also saw to it that everyone danced and matched couples for the waltz, schottische, quadrille, galop, and polka. While in other areas of the territory, the musicians might be paid in fresh meat, vegetables, hair cuts, clothing, or any other useable item, in Prescott all expenses were cash on the barrelhead. Often a reception for a visiting dignitary or special holiday supper dance with decorations and music would cost in excess of one thousand dollars, all of which was donated by subscription. No expense was spared. For example, when General William T. Sherman visited Fort Whipple in September 1878, he was feted at a breakfast hosted by Colonel Biddle of the post, a reception at the Courthouse, a reception at the quarters of General Wilcox, a reception at the Prescott Theater, and a farewell reception hosted by General and Mrs. Kautz. The *Miner* reported: "As the band struck up a march, those present were ushered to the ball-room, at the entrance of which each person was presented with a neat programme of the dances. Dancing commenced soon at 9 o'clock, at which hour the ladies passed to and fro presenting to the lookers-on a dazzling kaleidescopic picture of beauty and happiness. Mrs. Kautz wore white crepe du chene, elaborately trimmed with pink silk and lace; jewelry, diamonds. Mrs. Burmister, garnet silk and velvet, handsomely trimmed with lace and flowers; coal ornaments. Mrs. N. B. Bowers, tulle, with blue satin basque and trimmings, ornamented with blush roses, massive gold necklace and bracelets . . . ." and so on through twenty-two individual descriptions of the toilets of those ladies present. Speeches and toasts were numerous and the supper, usually served at midnight was always "the best ever seen in the territory up to this time."

Of course, there were also those quiet little evenings at home with a few close friends and because these events were less pretentious, they were probably more enjoyable. This gathering, held about 1898, included: (seated on floor, left to right) unidentified, Alice Day (stepdaughter of Dr. Warren E. Day), Clyde Watson, Pauline Schindler O'Neill, (seated on couch) unidentified, Elizabeth Smith, Agnes Conlon (cousin of Etta DeWitt), Eugene Brady O'Neill, unidentified, (standing) Agnes McCray, Etta DeWitt, unidentified, Joseph E. Morrison (attorney), Mabel Amanda Genung, William Owen "Bucky" O'Neill, unidentified.

William Owen "Bucky" O'Neill had served as sheriff, probate judge, editor of the Journal-Miner, *Captain of the Prescott Grays, owner-editor of* Hoof and Horn, *guide for the 1894 Smithsonian Institution expedition into the Grand Canyon, and mayor of Prescott. Bucky also penned a number of short stories which were published in various periodicals, but confided he could only write if Pauline played lilting Irish airs on the piano. Sometime after this photograph was taken, Bucky and other members of the First United States Volunteer Cavalry, nicknamed the "Rough Riders," left for Cuba to fight in the Spanish-American War. He was shot by a sniper on July 1, 1898, and on August 7 Pauline wrote to the* San Francisco Examiner: *"To those who will celebrate our nation's success, when your spirits are raised in triumph and your songs of thanksgiving are the loudest, remember that we, who sit and weep in our closed and darkened homes, have given our best gifts to our country and our flag. Patriotism, how many hearts are broken in thy cause?"*

In 1901 a short story by William O'Neill was found in the pigeon hole of someone's cluttered desk in the offices of Cosmopolitan *magazine. "Requiem of Drums" was printed in their February 1902*

edition, illustrated by Frederick Remington and featured with an adventurous tale by an Englishman named Rudyard Kipling and a preposterous science fiction fantasy about men on the moon by H. G. Wells. Photograph courtesy of the Department of Library, Archives and Public Records, State of Arizona

The basic supplies available for everyday meals were the same foodstuffs used to prepare banquets, teas, and receptions for special occasions. But the finishing touches which made the difference between plain and fancy fare were the festive delicacies prepared to accompany the repast. The more difficult and involved the preparation, the more unavailable or exotic the ingredients — the more desirable it became to make the function all the more notable.

Granny Dora Bubar's Watermelon Pickles

Yield: 12 to 14 quarts

2 watermelons with thick rind
Water to cover
About 1 cup of salt
First Cooking:
Alum (enough to pucker your mouth)
Water to cover

Second Cooking:
2 cups vinegar
2 cups sugar
A few cloves and cinnamon
Final Cooking:
1 quart Heinz cider vinegar
1 quart water
6 cups sugar
Some cinnamon and cloves

Peel and soak in weak salt water overnight. Next morning drain off salt water. Cook in weak alum water until color begins to turn. Drain from alum water and cook again in mixture of vinegar, sugar, cloves, and cinnamon. That can sit on stove all day simmering slowly. For final cooking add to mixture of Heinz cider vinegar, water, sugar, and some cinnamon and cloves. Set off and on stove for three or four days. *But do not cover!* As it cooks, the syrup becomes heavy. Put in jars — does not have to be sealed.

— Dora Rosenblatt Heap

Aunt "Mollie's" Watermelon Sweet Pickles

Yield: 6 to 7 quarts

White rind of 1 watermelon
1 teaspoon salt to each quart
  cold water

Syrup:
1 quart vinegar
1½ quarts sugar
Fruit, cinnamon, and cloves,
  as needed

Cut melon in small squares and add to salt and water. Cover and cook until soft, drain. Combine vinegar and sugar; boil to thicken. Add fruit, cinnamon, and cloves. Put in jars and seal.

— Mary Birchett Ruffner, wife of
Sheriff George C. Ruffner of Prescott

Watermelon Preserves

Yield: 3 quarts and one pint

White rind of ½ watermelon
Water enough to cover
Skin of 1 lemon
Syrup:
1 pound sugar for each

pound melon
1 teacup of water for each
  pound melon
1 lemon slice

Pare the rind and cut in cubes. Boil in water with skin of lemon to color them yellow. When tender take out in dishes. Make a syrup of sugar and water. When sugar is dissolved and hot, put in melon and lemon slice to flavor. Boil until melon looks transparent. Can while hot.

Arizona Citrus Marmalade

Yield: 8 to 10 glasses of jelly

2 oranges
2 lemons
2 grapefruit
2 cups water for every cup fruit

Equal amount of sugar to fruit
Pinch salt — will reduce amount
  of sugar needed to sweeten

Wash fruit; slice paper-thin strips with seeds into cheesecloth sack.

Soak 24 hours in water. Remove seeds. Cook uncovered until tender for about 1 hour and let stand until cool or overnight. Add sugar and salt to the fruit. Cook over low heat until thick. Pour into sterile jars at once.

~~~

Crystalized Fruit

2 cups sugar
1 cup water
¼ teaspoon cream of tartar

Orange sections, white grapes, cherries and any other fruit desired

Boil sugar with water and cream of tartar. Test it by dropping a little in cold water. When brittle, remove from fire. Dip into it sections of orange from which all skin is removed, white grapes, cherries, and any other fruit desired. Spread on waxed paper to harden.

~~~

Grape Ketchup

5 pounds ripe grapes
1 pint water
2½ pounds sugar
½ pint vinegar

1 tablespoon ground clove
1 tablespoon cinnamon
1 tablespoon allspice
Small amount salt and pepper

Put the grapes into a kettle with one pint of water; when warm, mash. Boil until the pulp is dissolved. Strain; add the other ingredients and boil until thick, being careful not to scorch. Serve with cold meats.

~~~

Cucumber Ketchup

Large ripe cucumbers
1 pint cider to each pint of drained pulp
2 tablespoons grated horseradish

2 tablespoons grated onion
2 teaspoons salt
½ teaspoon cayenne pepper

Pare cucumbers; remove seeds, grate, sprinkle with salt, and let drain overnight. To drained pulp, add required good cider vinegar, horseradish and onion, salt and cayenne pepper. Mix well; bottle, cork and seal by inserting the top of each bottle in hot melted beeswax and rosin, in the proportion of 1 quart rosin to 2 quarts beeswax.

Note: This ketchup requires no cooking and is excellent to serve with fish.

Banana Nut Tea Sandwiches

Bananas, one per person
Sponge cake
Fruit jelly, as needed

Mayonnaise, as needed
Nuts, as needed

Slice bananas in half and then lengthwise. Layer sponge cake with fruit jelly between the banana slices and hold with toothpicks. Mix mayonnaise with nuts and roll banana sandwiches in this until generously covered. Serve cold.

—From the diary of
Alice Butterfield

Gooseberry Shrub

6 quarts ripe gooseberries
1 quart cider vinegar
1 pound sugar to each pint juice

Place three quarts of ripe gooseberries in an earthen bowl, then pour over them a quart of good cider vinegar; let stand 24 hours; strain off the liquid and pour this over three quarts more of the fresh fruit. Allow this to stand the same length of time and strain as before. Add required sugar and boil twenty minutes. When cold, bottle and cork; serve on cracked ice.

Strawberry Shrub

1 quart strawberries
1 quart water
½ cup lemon juice

Sugar to taste
1 cup heavy cream

Mash strawberries and add water; strain through a cloth, then add lemon juice, sugar to suit, and freeze to a soft mush; then add cream and finish freezing; serve in thin glasses with berries on top for garnish.

Ephilet B. Gage made his fortune in mine speculation, primarily around Tombstone in the 1880s. In 1895 he built a mansion on the corner of Alarcon and East Gurley in Prescott. Six years later, the house was purchased by Frank Morrell Murphy, Gage's partner and a promoter of the railroad in Arizona. The Gage-Murphy mansion was built with the finest materials, including oak mantles on several of the six fireplaces. The solarium, or sun porch, displayed an ornate stained glass partition above its entrance. The dining room (foreground) was decorated with thick Oriental rugs, intricately patterned wallpaper, and a solid oak buffet which had been built in Chicago to the specifications of the owner. It was an altogether elegant setting for any social event, from afternoon teas to formal dinners. Photograph courtesy of Sharlot Hall Museum

White or Brown Bread

Yield: 2 loaves

½ pint boiling water
½ pint sweet milk
2 teaspoons salt

1 compressed yeast cake
Flour, as needed

Add boiling water to sweet milk. When partly cool, add salt and yeast cake which has been dissolved in warm water. Add flour for a light batter and let stand until early morning. Then add flour until it can be handled, and turn on a board and knead 20 minutes. Place in a dish and let rise until doubled in bulk, or about 3 hours. Mold into loaves and let rise until doubled in bulk, or about 1 hour. Bake at 350 degrees F. for 45 minutes or until browned.

Note: To make brown bread, whole wheat flour is used instead of white flour.

Almond Biscuits

Yield: 3 to 4 dozen

1 egg, well beaten
Essence of almond
½ pound (2 cups) dry sifted flour

¼ pound (¾ cup) confectioners' sugar
¼ pound (1 stick) butter

Icing:

½ pound (1½ cups) confectioners' sugar
1 egg white, well beaten

2 tablespoonfuls water
½ cup chopped almonds
3 drops essence of almond

Preheat oven to 425 degrees F. Add egg and a few drops of essence of almond to flour, ¼ pound of confectioners' sugar, and butter rubbed together until well creamed. Roll out on floured board until quite thin. Cut with biscuit cutter and bake until browned. Remove from the oven and when cold, cover each biscuit with icing. Place in refrigerator until icing hardens.

To make icing, combine sugar, egg white, water, almonds, and almond essence. Blend well.

Note: An icing can also be made of confectioners' sugar and a teaspoon or two of evaporated milk. If too thin, add more confectioners' sugar until it is of spreading consistency. (Icing will be somewhat thick to stir.)

Henry Brinkmeyer, Sr. was born in Germany in 1866 and emigrated to America at the age of seventeen to avoid conscription in the German army. At first he worked as a baker at the Scopel Hotel, located on the southwest corner of Goodwin and Montezuma. In the November 29, 1887 issue of the Prescott Morning Courier was an announcement that Henry and a partner had taken charge of a new bakery and lunch stand located a few doors north of Kelly and Stephens mercantile store on the northwest corner of Gurley and Montezuma. He did so well that within a few years he owned the Brinkmeyer Hotel, where Henry, his wife, Ina Muzick Brinkmeyer, and their children, Henry, Jr. and Marcella, lived.

Henry's enterprises continued to grow. According to his youngest daughter, Caroline, he bartered meals and lodging in exchange for fresh produce, eggs, meat, and milk needed by the bakery and restaurant. Soon he began a delivery route for the bakery, using a closed wagon and two horses — one to deliver to the west side of town and the other to deliver to the east side of town. He had an interest in the brick factory, the ice plant, and the brewery, and his fortune was assured. So Henry decided that it was time for his family to have a house of their own. Of course, the prosperous citizens of Prescott were building fancy homes all the time, but the Brinkmeyer house caused a bit of a sensation. It arrived in sections from a lumber yard in Los Angeles, prefabricated and ready to be quickly erected on a substantial stone foundation. Within the year, it was all that he owned.

The fire of July 14, 1900 destroyed both the Brinkmeyer Hotel and Bakery along with over eighty other businesses in the downtown. Fort Whipple offered Henry the use of their ovens so that he could continue to bake his rolls, breads, pies, and cakes. "Bought'n" bread was considered as good a treat as candy by the citizens, and Henry's were the best to be found. In the July 17 issue of the Arizona Weekly Journal-Miner Henry Brinkmeyer announced that while his loss had been considerable, with little of it covered by insurance, Henry would begin immediately the erection of a new hotel built of brick on the site of the old wooden hotel which had been burned to the ground. The hotel, shown here, was finished in 1901.

The bakery and restaurant were reopened in the basement of the new hotel. Here customers could order Sunday chicken dinner with all the trimmings for twenty-five cents and take home pastries, pies, cookies, or bread hot from the oven and wrapped in paper (on the counter, far left). Shown in this photograph taken shortly after the Brinkmeyer hotel, bakery, and restaurant reopened, are Uncle August, (left), Henry's brother who came from Germany at the turn of the century, and the proprietor, Henry Brinkmeyer, Sr., who ran it until his death in 1941. Hotel exterior courtesy of the Department of Library, Archives and Public Records, State of Arizona

132

Bakery Interior courtesy of Sharlot Hall Museum

Roll Jelly Cake

1½ cups flour
2 level teaspoons baking powder
4 eggs, separated

1 cup sugar
½ cup milk
½ cup favorite jelly

Preheat oven to 375 degrees F. Sift flour and baking powder together; beat yolks of eggs until light, then add sugar, beating thoroughly; then add milk; then gradually add flour and baking powder. Beat egg whites until stiff. Fold the egg whites into the batter. Pour into well-buttered long, shallow tins and bake for 15 minutes. Turn out on a damp towel on a bread board, cover top with jelly, and roll up carefully while warm.

Coffee Cake

¾ cup butter,
  at room temperature
1 cup sugar
1 cup molasses
1 teaspoon cinnamon
½ teaspoon ground cloves

½ teaspoon nutmeg
½ teaspoon salt
1½ teaspoons baking soda
1 cup strong coffee
5 cups flour
1 cup raisins

Preheat oven to 350 degrees F. Cream butter and sugar; add molasses, cinnamon, cloves, nutmeg, and salt. Dissolve baking soda in coffee and add to the mixture. Beat in flour and raisins. Batter should be stiff. Add more coffee or put in less flour, if necessary. Pour batter into a buttered pan and bake for about 35 minutes or until golden brown.

Note: Icing for almond biscuits can also be used for coffee cake. Nuts can be sprinkled on top.

Strawberry Layer Cake No. 1

3 eggs, separated
½ cup (1 stick) butter
1 cup sugar

2 cups flour
½ cup milk
1 teaspoon baking powder

Icing:
1 cup powdered sugar
1 egg white
1 quart strawberries

Preheat oven to 350 degrees F. Beat the yolks of the eggs well; add the butter and sugar, beat in a part of the flour; mix in the milk, then add the remaining flour with the baking powder in it. Beat the egg whites until stiff. Fold egg whites into batter. Bake in 2 layer pans about 25 minutes or until a broom straw comes out of cake clean.

To make icing, gradually add sugar to the egg white beating with a spoon. Spread on each layer of the cake. Just before serving, sweeten and partly crush 1 quart strawberries; put them on top of 1 layer and place the other layer on top.

Strawberry Layer Cake No. 2

1 to 3 cups butter, at room
   temperature
1½ cups sugar
½ cup strained strawberry juice

2 cups flour
¼ teaspoon baking soda
4 to 5 eggs, separated

Icing:

1 cup sugar
3 tablespoons strawberry juice

2 tablespoons water
1 egg white, whipped

Preheat oven to 375 degrees F. Heat the bowl first, then cream the butter, sugar and egg yolks. Add strawberry juice. Sift the flour with the soda and add it to the bowl. (The acid juice will render cream of tartar unnecessary.) Stiffly whip egg whites, and fold into the batter. Bake in buttered layer tins for 25 minutes or until cake tests done. When cool spread each layer except one with a soft icing.

To make icing, boil sugar with juice and water. When it threads, pour it over the whipped white of egg and beat it a little before putting on the cake.

English Walnut Cake

Yield: 3 large layers or 4 small ones

2 eggs
1 cup thin sweet cream
1 scant cup sugar

2 teaspoons baking powder
Flour, as needed

Cream Filling:

½ cup rich sweet milk
½ cup sugar
1 heaping teaspoon flour

Cold milk
Chopped English walnut meats
   to taste

Preheat oven to 375 degrees F. Break eggs in a large cup and beat; then fill the cup with thin, sweet cream; pour in a mixing bowl and add water, baking powder, and flour enough to make a batter that will pour. Bake in layer pans for 25 minutes or until cake tests done.

For the cream filling, boil together the milk and sugar; moisten the flour with a little cold milk and add to the boiling milk and sugar. When it has cooled slightly, spread between the layers and sprinkle each layer generously with chopped English walnut meats. Frost top and sides and arrange a few walnut halves over top. Set in oven a moment to harden frosting.

Getting to their destination in the territory was only part of the many problems faced by early settlers. Once they arrived, houses had to be built, land cleared and planted, and arrangements made to secure supplies not made or grown locally.

Sam and Jacob Miller were the first to establish a freighting business in the Prescott area, and they were soon joined by several others who felt that the profits outweighed the enormous risks involved. The arrival of pack mules or a wagon train carrying provisions was such an important event that the *Arizona Miner* listed what supplies had been received by which mercantile store in the pages of the newspaper, and local citizens made note of the occasion in diaries and letters. Josephine Stephens, whose father was a partner in Kelly and Stephens store, wrote in her journal entry of June 30, 1879: "I got my bottle of Glycerine up to Goldwaters." "Grapes and Peaches in town" she wrote on July 25, and on October 13 "We got our new winter hats up to Kelly and Stephens Will [Kelly] bought them in San Francisco."

According to bills and receipts collected by Sharlot Hall, the shopping list of James Alexander included:

2 Cream Tartar	2.50
2 lbs. Brown Sugar	1.00
2 lbs. Tea	3.00
4 Plugs Tobacco	2.00
16 lbs. Beans	4.25
1 pair Pants	3.50
1 pair Butts and Screws	.75
1 Lock	1.00
1 Pipe	1.00
1 bottle Mustard	.50

His order was filled at Bowers and Brothers on July 22, 1866. Alexander had an account there, so others could also bring his list in to the store for him. On one occasion, $5.88 was charged to Alexander's account for "2 bars soap, 1 box Pain Killer, and $4.00 cash." It was often the case that the mercantile provided banking services, and stores generally had a scale to weigh gold dust and nuggets. Livestock, fresh produce, eggs, and other goods were also taken in trade.

Bashford and Burmister, referred to more commonly as the B and B, was one of the largest stores in the area and served the entire northern portion of Arizona. The operation started out rather modestly but by the end of 1894 a second and third floor had been added to their building on Gurley Street. The *Arizona Weekly Journal-Miner* reported in their February 20, 1895 edition: "Next week the Bashford-Burmister Co. expect to have their elevator in operation. This is the first instance of the introduction of this device in Prescott of an improved nature, and when in running order will serve three floors of this mammoth establishment. Water will be the motive power used."

Five years later, the B and B was one of the buildings lost in the fire of July 14, 1900. When the structure burned to the ground, along with about eighty other businesses downtown, the Bank of Arizona — in temporary quarters there while waiting for completion of a new office — lost all their records. The library reading room, which had been utilizing space in the store, also lost everything.

This photograph shows the B and B about 1903 after it was rebuilt on the same site, facing the Plaza. By 1904 they again carried every item imaginable: yard goods, groceries, hardware, union suits, mining supplies, window shades, Studebaker automobiles, drugs and patent medicines, furniture, stoves, dishes, ladies' hose (sold by size), pots and pans, blankets and rugs, Indian curios, boots and shoes, clothes for every member of the family, and much more. Photograph courtesy of Sharlot Hall Museum

Downtown Prescott was rebuilt after the fire of 1900. Looking west on Gurley, stores (including the B and B) are visible from Cortez to Montezuma on the right hand side of the street. On the left is the Hotel Burke (later called Hotel St. Michael), a fruit wagon passing down Cortez Street on the right side of the Plaza, the new Bank of Arizona building, and to the far left is the office of Wright's Prescott Electric Company where the Bank conducted its business after the fire. The safe against the wall of the telephone office could possibly be the same one rescued from the smoldering embers of the B and B. The Bank's assets had been protected from incineration inside the safe, but officials couldn't get it through the door of the telephone company so it was left out on the sidewalk, where it was business as usual.

In January 1903, about the time of this photograph, a letter to the editor appeared in the page of the Prescott Courier suggesting that Thumb Butte (seen in the distance) be renamed because it was "the scene of one of the earliest tragedies happening in the early settlement of this section by the whites. In the year 1864 Mr. Alexander went out to its vicinity in search of a horse which had strayed away from town. Failing to return in proper time, a party was made up to go in search of him. The searching party followed his tracks to where he was jumped by Indians and then by the arrows along his line of retreat to the foot of the butte, where they found his dead body. It would seem fitting that this butte should bear the name of the man who baptised it with his blood. viz, 'Alexander's Butte.' (signed) Pioneer." Photograph courtesy of the Department of Library, Archives and Public Records, State of Arizona

Although the buildings on the southeast corner of Cortez and Gurley were not demolished, they did sustain some damage. Looking down Gurley (top left) is the Yavapai Club; the house lived in by John and Jessie Fremont during the time they lived in Prescott while he served as fifth territorial governor; the lot where the Elks built their opera house and lodge rooms; the electric company; a milliner's shop and the Gurley street entrance to the New York Store; the Bank of Arizona; the main entrance on Cortez street for the New York Store; and the Knights of Pythias building — at forty-six feet, one of the territory's first skyscrapers!

Sometime after this photograph was taken, the Fremont house was moved to Union Street to make room for the first Carnegie Library built in Arizona. Meanwhile, the Woman's Club of Prescott (now the Monday Club) used the basement of the bank to operate a Free Reading Room staffed by members of their library committee. Later on, the Boy Scouts occupied the bank's basement.

Apparently, not all of Prescott's assets were entrusted to the Bank of Arizona, the first of its kind to be chartered in the territory. The Phoenix Gazette announced: "Prescott, A. T. is now the nearest approach to the New Jerusalem, as it is described in Holy Writ, as the streets are being paved with gold. It is true it is not of a degree of fineness equal to that to be found in the next world, but it is the best that can be done on this mundane sphere.

"Gold, however, is one of the ingredients of the granite pavement used in the 'city among the pines,' and one may not be surprised some day if the panicky times shoudl ever reach that locality, to see the pavement run through a quartz mill to secure the gold that might be extracted by the leaching process.

"Each ton of the rock used contains $4.00 in gold and 20 cents in silver, and this typical mining city enjoys the proud distinction of being the only one in the world with golden streets." Photograph courtesy of the Department of Library, Archives and Public Records, State of Arizona

Richard Cunningham McCormick, Secretary of State for the newly-created Arizona Territory, brought over three hundred volumes from the East in the wagons of Governor Goodwin's party to serve as a reference library for officials and legislators. Several months later, on May 30, 1864 a dispute arose during the first town meeting because a suitable name for the territorial capital could not be agreed upon. Several were proposed, but there was not a majority for any of them, so Richard McCormick advised that the settlement be named after the renowned historian, William Hickling Prescott, who wrote one of the most popular books in the territorial library, *The History of the Conquest of Mexico.*

Librarian Henry W. Fleury reported in the March 28, 1866 *Arizona Miner* that the collection consisted of 309 volumes as of September 1, 1865, and he called for all checked-out books to be returned forthwith — perhaps the first official overdue notice in the territory. Included in the inventory were several dozen encyclopedias, Spanish and English dictionaries, a large collection of law books, U.S. Census reports, maps, surveys made by the Smithsonian Institution, almanacs, and a wide variety of informational material on such diverse topics as Indians, early expeditions into the Southwest and Mexico, botany, and mineral identification.

Other titles, such as *Pilgrim's Progress, Paradise Lost, the Holy Bible, Robinson Crusoe, Camels For Military Purposes, Lewis On Weak Lungs,* and *Tale Of A Tub* reflected the desire for culture, sense of adventure, and whimsical humor of Prescott's early settlers.

In 1870 a group of ladies interested in the cultural advancement of Prescott organized a library association and opened a reading room on Cortez Street which provided 263 books collected from local households and fifty out-of-town newspapers. Their efforts may very well have been in response to the editorial of John Marion who suggested in the April 2, 1870 edition of the *Arizona Miner:* "Prescott is a young town, and a small one, yet, we think it is high time our people were taking some steps towards founding a public library here. A public library is a big card for any town, and the establishment of one here could not fail to benefit residents and strangers.

"If our citizens think as we do, that it is time to move in this matter, we ask some of them to start the ball in motion. A town so isolated as ours is, should have something besides games of chance to amuse and instruct the citizens."

The Prescott Literary and Dramatic Association formed in 1876 to hold discussions, excluding religious and political subjects, and to establish a public reading room. On February 2, 1877 they opened their doors, but soon that attempt also went the way of the earlier library association. For the next fifteen years, library facilities consisted only of those provided privately through individuals. Then on August 19, 1895 the Woman's Club of Prescott was organized.

Sarah Shivers Fisher (insert), later the wife of Mayor Morris Goldwater, was one of the founders and served on their first library committee board. For the next five years they worked tirelessly to establish a free public library. With the promise of matching funds from Andrew Carnegie, all seemed within their grasp. But, like so many other endeavours, their hopes were snuffed out by Prescott's great fire. The only help accepted by local citizens in rebuilding the stricken city were donations toward the four thousand dollars needed to secure the Carnegie endowment. At last, on November 24, 1903 the Prescott Public Library opened its doors.

Although this was a free library, in that a fee was no longer charged to borrow books, the thirteen hundred publications which were available were handled carefully by the club volunteers who staffed it. Caroline Brinkmeyer explains: "First you went to the card catalog to see what book you wanted and then asked the librarian for it." A library patron is shown in this rare view being assisted in that very way. It was not until 1914 that the first paid librarian, Mrs. Emerson, was employed. Bessie Bork also assisted at the library for many years. Photograph of Carnegie library interior courtesy of the author. Insert of Sarah Shivers Fisher courtesy of Sharlot Hall Museum

With the rich gold discoveries in the central mountains of Arizona and the establishment of the territorial capital in Prescott, came a wave of emigrants to settle the area. And along with those hardy and adventuresome pioneers came one of Arizona's first tourists! J. Ross Browne, a journalist from San Francisco, visited the territory for several months in 1863 to 64 and later wrote about his tour for Harper's New Monthly Magazine.

Indeed, Arizona seemed to attract attention from all quarters. Early explorers of the area commented on their surroundings. No matter how difficult the privations, those who crossed Arizona mountains were awed by their rugged beauty, and, even then, nothing could compare with the desert sunsets.

The automobile made the territory even more accessible. Of course, this wonderful new form of travel had its drawbacks. A traveler had to dress properly; pack plenty of food and water, spare auto parts, tools and other supplies; and have a good idea where to find a gas station. At first, fuel was not pumped but came in barrels packed two to a wooden case, and if no gas station was available, one could usually buy fuel at the local general store. Driving in the desert could provide a number of new experiences like losing track of the road and getting bogged down in sand. But to those who felt the territory had become a bit too civilized, the automobile opened new avenues of adventure.

This photograph of a Prescott-to-Tucson motorcade was taken on April 22, 1904 on Washington Street in Phoenix. Prescott participants include (second from the right) Frank W. Foster, Mrs. Foster, and daughter Blanche; in the auto second from the left are Alex Lyons and W. C. Miller; in the third automobile are O. A. Hesla and Mrs. Hesla; and fifth in line are H. D. Aitken and Mrs. Aitken.

For a few enterprising souls, driving a Studebaker, Maxwell, Winton, Franklin, Pierce-Arrow, Knox, or Packard was not a great enough thrill. Caroline Brinkmeyer remembers the brother of Nellie von Gerichten Smith purchasing a "knocked down" automobile. It was a one seater with no roof — and little of anything else. All the parts came in boxes, and he then put the machine together from scratch, bolting the body in place, installing the engine and putting on the wheels. It caused both astonishment and admiration when the finished product actually ran! Photograph courtesy of the Department of Library, Archives and Public Records, State of Arizona

Dependable transportation was always a problem in Arizona, and the coming of the railroad had probably the greatest impact on territorial lifestyles of any event during the settling of the southwestern United States. Along the rails came ever increasing numbers of new settlers, bringing with them ideas, attitudes, and energy. The mineral and agricultural bounty of the territory could now be transported to additional and more distant markets, and the new prosperity this generated filled box cars with more modern home furnishings, more fashionable clothing, and the finest in foodstuffs. But the railroad affected to an even larger degree the lives of area Indians. In the 1880s, when the Santa Fe railroad began featuring Indians in advertisements for the first time, their lifestyle changed drastically. Suddenly there was a fervent interest in these native peoples' relics and customs. In order to meet the demand for Indian-made items, pottery, baskets, and blankets began appearing with motifs the makers felt would be more appealing to Anglo tastes. The pots, baskets, and figurines being sold by this Maricopa woman in April 1907 were more decorative than those normally used in everyday circumstances. Photograph courtesy of Sharlot Hall Museum

In 1879 the dean of Indian traders, J. Lorenzo Hubbell, established his trading post at Ganado on the Navajo Reservation. He took a keen interest in business dealings with the Navajo and Hopi Indians, and his honest and gracious lifestyle among primitive surroundings — his home on the reservation contained a large library and rare paintings, some of which had been brought by his mother from Toledo, Spain — earned him the nickname "Don" Lorenzo.

Hubbell is shown here, circa 1890s, with his wife, Lina Rubic Hubbell, and their children Adela, Barbara, Lorenzo Jr., and Ramon. Although he had acquired only nineteen months of formal education, Hubbell was appointed sheriff of Apache County and in 1912 was elected senator to the first state legislature.

Because of his fascination with the lore and utility of the traditional Navajo blanket (which was painstakenly hand woven by the women from wool they had carded from their sheep and then spun and dyed), Lorenzo Hubbell was the first to suggest that they could be used as rugs due to their beauty and durability. This unique approach created a national market which still flourishes.

Today the Hubbell Trading Post is designated a National Historic Site. Photograph courtesy of Sharlot Hall Museum

Alice Butterfield Hewins and an unidentified gentleman watch with some curiosity as a Hopi snake priest enters a kiva, or sacred underground chamber. This photograph, unposed and taken with unsophisticated equipment, is a rare view made around 1907.

The religious ceremonies of the Hopi included their snake dance, during which participants carried the "little brothers" in their mouths before releasing these reptiles as messengers to the gods with their prayers for rain and abundant crops. Anglo onlookers sometimes forgot the sacred nature of the occasion and would speak or laugh loudly, take photographs, or make sketches and otherwise interfere with the conduct of the ceremonies. Over the years, the patience of their Hopi hosts wore thin, and only those visitors who behave with quiet respect and whose attendance does not impede the natural progression of events are welcome on the mesas. Photograph courtesy of the Department of Library, Archives and Public Records, State of Arizona

Sharlot Mabridth Hall (right) and her long-time friend, Alice Butterfield Hewins, are shown visiting Montezuma Castle, named by early settlers in the Verde Valley who mistakenly believed it had been built by Aztec Indians. These Sinagua "apartment houses," which stood five stories high and had once been occupied by as many as two hundred people, were still accessible to sightseers in 1907. The climb was strenuous and many of the rooms are quite high above Beaver Creek, which may account for the rope tied under Mrs. Hewins' arms. Photograph courtesy of the Department of Library, Archives and Public Records, State of Arizona

The Grand Canyon has always been Arizona's most spectacular natural wonder. Perhaps just as colorful was John Hance, one of the Canyon's first tourist guides. He had a ranch on the south rim in the 1880s, and guests were entertained by trips down a primitive trail to Bright Angel Creek along with a generous dose of John's tall tales. His most popular story was that he had dug the Grand Canyon himself —as a mining venture!

This photograph was taken on June 10, 1907 and, in addition to the trail guides, includes the entire graduating class of Prescott High School. From left to right are Orange McNeil, Grace Shank, Orpha Haisley, and Ruby Loy.

Twelve years later the Grand Canyon was established as a national park. Photograph courtesy of Sharlot Hall Museum

147

This photograph was taken by Will R. Beatty of Prescott in what looks like a quarry — perhaps the one which used to be in Miller Valley. The subjects are beautifully attired, yet their plainest accessory is perhaps the most interesting. You may notice that both these lovely lasses are carrying umbrellas, although they already wear wide brimmed hats and light weight dresses, and no other gear for inclement weather is visible. The answer is simple.

Makeup used by women a century ago had a wax base to add a translucent effect to the face. If one got too near the heat of a fireplace or in the direct sun, soon the shape of things very definitely took a turn for the worse. In addition to utilitarian umbrellas, this cosmetic quandary sparked the popularity of the more decorative parasol, the sun shade (which looked like a parasol but could easily be tilted to the side), and hand-held face screens, which looked something like flat fans. Photograph courtesy of Sharlot Hall Museum

Natural Cosmetics

Cosmetic concoctions, like home remedies, were often based on Indian lore and a knowledge of the more unusual uses of vegetables, flowers, and other plants. In such a harsh environment, preparations to protect skin and hair were more a necessity than a luxury.

As the Arizona territory became a more habitable place, beauty treatments and fashionable attire became the hallmarks of those who had secured their fortune, and these trends were imitated by others who hoped to give that impression.

No claims are made for the effectiveness of these natural cosmetics. Although they were generally in use a hundred years ago, we strongly suggest that, as with all cosmetic treatments, you use them with the utmost care. The simplest way to test for any allergic reaction is to apply each preparation on a small patch of skin on the inside of your wrist before using it in larger quantities or on other parts of your body. You should use only fresh ingredients and keep their containers and your work area as clean as possible. It is not advisable to return unused preparations to storage jars; make and apply only what you need at the time.

Citrus Refresher: A hundred years ago, bathtubs looked more like large metal buckets. It was impossible to bathe both the top half and the bottom half at the same time. The free-standing model had a tendency to tip over if not properly entered and exited, or if too much water or a brawny bather made them top-heavy. Charles O. "Charlie" Brown, owner of the opulent Congress Hall Saloon in Tucson, brought the first privately-owned bathtub to that town. It was zinc and said to be a caution, as most bathing was done in public bath houses, hotels, and horse troughs. Bathing under those circumstances was not the luxurious, leisurely process that it later became.

You can pamper yourself whenever you take the time for a long, hot soak in the bathtub by adding thin slices of one or more fresh lemons as you run the water into the tub. The lemon helps remove the oil and perspiration from your skin without drying it out. In addition, the bathroom smells delightful and the aroma is very refreshing.

Hair Tonic: An approved hair tonic consists of sixty grams of quinine to an ounce of vaseline. When the hair is thin and dry this application will give the nourishment necessary to keep it glossy and usually prevents it from coming out. For a dry scalp equal parts of the best French brandy and coconut oil rubbed thoroughly on the roots three or four times a week is also a safe tonic and nutriment.

"**Hair Grower:** Plain vaseline, the yellow product, rubbed into the scalp nightly or several times a week will prevent your hair from coming out and also induce a new growth. It is not a new remedy, for it is well known that the petroleum has a wonderful effect on the growth of the hair. Many of the Irish girls who come to this country with such fine heads of hair owe the growth to kerosene, it is said, which is a favorite remedy for strengthening the hair follicles in Ireland. But as that is unpleasant to use, the vaseline comes next in order, possessing much the same properties. An Ivory soap shampoo once a month, thorough rinsing, and clean comb and brush are also necessary, to keep hair and scalp in good condition."

—From the scrapbook of
Nellie von Gerichten Smith

Tooth Wash: A few drops of lemon juice in plain water is an excellent tooth wash. It not only removes the tartar, but sweetens the breath.

Breath Freshner: If a sprig of parsley dipped in vinegar is eaten after an onion, no unpleasant odor from the breath can be detected.

A cup of strong coffee will also remove onion odor from breath.

Getting Rid of Freckles: Let some grated horseradish stand in a dish of cold buttermilk or sour milk overnight. Strain and apply the mixture every morning and evening.

Some women bleached freckles by applying a mixture of the juice of one lemon with as much sugar as possible. This was done several times a day and applied with a camel's hair brush.

Other women who did not have such concoctions available to them, bleached their freckles by wearing wet baby diapers draped over their arms and hands. This procedure was also supposed to ease sunburn pain.

A tan, which indicated a rough outdoor life, could be removed by applying a mixture of buttermilk and sour cream several nights in a row or throughout the day.

To Banish Warts: Wrap up over night in a poultice made of lemon juice and fine table salt until the wart disappears. Two applications on a seed wart left the place very sore, but when healed the wart was gone. This is also good for corns. It works the same way as with warts.

Warts disappeared after several applications of the "tobacco spit" of grasshoppers.

Manicure Acid: The finest of manicure acids is made by putting a teaspoonful of lemon juice in a cupful of warm water. This removes most stains from the fingers and nails and loosens the cuticle more satisfactorily than can be done by the use of a sharp instrument.

Fingernails: "The study of fingernails, the shape and color of which are said to indicate certain traits of character, is a new occupation. Long and slender fingernails denote imagination, love of art, and laziness; if long and flat, they are the sign of prudence, good sense and grave mental faculties; if wide and short, of anger and rudeness, controversy and obstinacy. A healthy color signifies virtue, health, happiness, courage, and liberality; dry and brittle nails are signs of anger, cruelty, quarrel, culminating even to murder; curved in the shape of claws, hypocrisy and wickedness; if soft, feebleness of body and mind; and lastly, we are told that short nails, gnawed down to the flesh, signify silliness and dissipation."

From an untitled newspaper clipping
dated 1884 in the scrapbook of
Nellie von Gerichten Smith

Chapped Hands: Apply vinegar or lemon juice often, mixed with honey and lard to cure extreme roughness.

A bucket of corn meal or oats was kept in the kitchen so you could put your hands in it after wet or cold jobs to keep hands from chapping. Soften with lamb's fat, mutton tallow, linseed, or olive oil.

Aunt Emily Brinkmeyer's Hand Lotion

1 to 4 ounces of tragacanth
(Note: sometimes called "white leaf," this plant gum comes in white translucent flakes which swell up in water and act as an emulsifier. Check with your pharmacist.)
4 ounces of glycerine
4 ounces of witch hazel
1 pint rain water, strained and boiled
5 cents of rosewater, enough to scent lotion

Soak gum tragacanth in water until dissolved. Shake this mixture up and then add the rest of the ingredients. If the lotion is too thick, add 4 ounces more of witch hazel.

This was used by the Brinkmeyer family for decades with good results.

Foot Powder: Mix ½ cup corn starch with 2 teaspoons baking soda and apply to feet and shoes. The corn starch absorbs moisture, and the baking soda helps control foot odor.

Wrinkle Remover: Stir one ounce melted white wax, two ounces strained honey, and two ounces juice of lily bulbs together and rub into the wrinkles.

Ella W. Webb, postmistress at Cline in the Tonto Basin from November 25, 1891 to January 17, 1905, used corn meal mixed with egg white and a little water as a facial cleanser. The corn meal helped loosen dry skin, and the egg white tightened the face. Marian Webb (Armer) Schmidt remembers: "Mother would look in the mirror, and if she saw any wrinkles, she'd use this to draw them."

Instructions on *How a Pug Nose May be Given a More Stylish Form* from an untitled newspaper, circa 1880s, in the scrapbook of Nellie von Gerichten Smith.

"The nose is simply a piece of cartilage, and its shape can be changed with ease. A clever Frenchman, some years ago, invented a machine for that purpose, and I have heard made a fortune by it. So many people are troubled with noses whose shapes do not please their owners or their owner's friends. The machine consisted of a small shell in two parts, hinged together. It is made of iron japanned or enameled. It is in shape inside that of a perfectly moulded nose, according to the type of the features of the wearer. Thus you can obtain a Roman, Grecian, retrousee, aquiline or any other shape you desire. To apply the instrument the nose is first bathed in warm water at bedtime and thoroughly heated and softened. Then it is well greased with olive oil, glycerine, vaseline or other oily substance. Finally the nose-improver is fixed on and both sides clasped together and the wearer keeps it on all night, taking care in the morning to wash in cold water only. It is a rather painful process at first, but after the first two or three applications of the improver there is no more trouble. In about a month the nose begins to take its new shape, and at the end of from eight to ten weeks the alteration is said to be perfect and permanent — that is, until the patient becomes tired of that particular shape and is desirous of having another, when the same operation with another instrument is necessitated. I have known people who change their noses four or five times in as many years. In that way a man could change the style of his nose as often as he changed the cut of his trousers."

How to Reduce One's Weight

"A woman weighing 200 pounds called on a physician for advice. He gave her the following instructions:

1. For breakfast eat a piece of beef or mutton as large as your hand, with a slice of white bread twice as large. For dinner the same amount of meat, or if preferred, fish or poultry, with the same amount of farinaceous or vegetable food in the form of bread or potato. For supper nothing.

2. Drink only when greatly annoyed with thirst; than a mouthful of lemonade without sugar.

3. Take three times a week some form of bath in which there shall be immense perspiration. The Turkish bath is best. You must work, either in walking or some other way, several hours a day.

4. You must rise early in the morning and retire late at night. Much sleep fattens people.

5. The terrible corset you have on, which compresses the center of the body, making you look a good deal fatter than you really are, must be taken off, and you must have a corset which any dressmaker can fit to you — a corset for the lower part of the abdomen — which will raise this great mass and support you.

She followed the advice for six months, and trained herself down to 152 pounds."

—From the scrapbook of
Nellie von Gerichten Smith

Fat All My Life, and How I Got Rid Of It

"First a captivating plumpness begins to steal upon woman in her twenties. Plumpness is followed by — oh, horrors! — fatness and shortness of breath, and heart flutters. Then, alas, comes the chin that is double and the comical lumbering waddle of the overfat. Fine sarcasm to tell such a woman to exercise. Why not counsel flying? She is as able to do the one as the other. It's another keen cut to suggest dieting. When ladies are just so fat they haven't an ounce of will power or energy to spare for extras — just living is hard enough work for them.

What then? Are these unfortunates condemned to be fat for life? No, believe it or not; a simple home recipe easy to get at a drug store will take that fat off and keep it off. Listen!

½ ounce Marmola
½ ounce Fluid Extract Cascara Aromatic
3½ ounces Syrup Simplex

mixed at home and taken in teaspoonful doses after meals and at bedtime will take off as much as a pound a day in some cases. Get the Marmola in the sealed packages — you are sure it is fresh that way — take the mixture a month, and you'll see. The fat seems to drop off and leave nice, smooth, firm flesh, while the health and complexion improve wonderfully.''

From an untitled newspaper advertisement,
circa 1880s in the Journal of
Nellie von Gerichten Smith

Advice To Girls from the scrapbook of Nellie von Gerichten Smith, circa 1880s.

''Somebody gives the following advice to girls. It is worth volumes of fiction and sentimentalism:

Men who are worth having want women for wives. A bundle of gewgaws, bound with a string of flats and quivers, sprinkled with cologne and set in a carmine saucet — this is no help for a man who expects to raise a family of boys on veritable bread and meat. The piano and lace frames are good in their places, and so are ribbons, frills and tinsels; but you cannot make a dinner of the former, nor a bed blanket of the latter — and awful as may seem such an idea to you, both dinner and bed blankets are necessary to domestic happiness. Life has its realities, as well as fancies, but you make it all decorations, remembering the tassels and curtains, but forgetting the bedstead. Suppose a man of good sense, and of course good prospects, to be looking for a wife, what chance have you to be chosen? You may cap him, or you may trap him, or catch him, but how much better to make it an object for him to catch you. Render yourself worthy of catching and you will need no shrewd mother or brother to help you find a market.''

Fashion Notes

The Arizona Territory, although isolated from civilization and its social influences, nevertheless was affected by fashion and all that it represented. After basic needs were met, settlements developed an inner society of those who were influential, affluent and — above all — fashionable. Increased leisure time and easier accessibility of materials and information helped to increase the tempo in vying for the unofficial title of "best dressed," and women went to unbelieveable lengths to outdo each other at each social function.

Although changes made in the female form were thought drastic enough to be ridiculed in this untitled newspaper cartoon, every woman who expected to stay in style followed suit when the exaggerated bustle was overthrown by the "hourglass figure," featuring ballooning sleeves and wider skirts to accentuate the tightly corseted waist. And they never even drew a deep breath when the "leg of mutton" sleeve look shifted forward to produce the newly-touted "pouter pigeon" silhouette which pushed the rib cage forward and held the neck erect with the addition of boned collars.

To those pioneering women who remembered reluctantly putting aside their silks and satins because calicos and ginghams were better suited to the hostile Arizona wilderness, it was of great importance to reflect all the best that civilization offered by wearing the most opulent apparel available. But Arizona's daughters had no such memories, and to them it was more important to dress in comfortable attire that would allow them to participate more fully in activities outside the home. Strict adherence to domesticity and the highly visible social structures established by Arizona's pioneer women was under attack and fashion fired the first volley. Newspaper cartoon from the scrapbook of Nellie von Gerichten Smith

155

Although the first American based company for the exclusive manufacture of bicycles was not established until 1878, the May 22, 1869 edition of the Arizona Miner *carried the following "Three concise rules for velocipede riders: straddle, paddle, skedaddle!"*

By the 1890s safety bicycles with both wheels of equal size and rubber, air-filled tires became popular as an adult conveyance. This pastime prompted ladies' fashions to adapt to the requirements of proper yet pretty attire, including the acceptance of appearing publicly in pants — a garment abhorred and ridiculed in earlier years. Snappy songs popularized both the style and mobility of the bicycle age.

Only with the advent of the automobile, and the new wave of fashionable "motor garments" generated by it, did the bicycle craze wane. Adults, like these Phoenix residents, gave their "bikes" to the children, and soon its importance to the older generation was all but forgotten. Photograph courtesy of the Department of Library, Archives and Public Records, State of Arizona

During the Civil War, some military shoes became available in a left and right style, but people by and large preferred shoes made to fit either foot. They were easier to put on because one didn't have to be concerned with which foot went in which shoe, and economically they were a much better idea because a person could buy just one shoe to replace the one which had worn out. These people could not imagine throwing away both shoes just because one wore out faster!

A. J. Mason was one of Prescott's most proficient boot and shoe makers during the 1880s. While he used cow hide for most of the styles he manufactured, in San Francisco customers could select other types of leather according to the use of the shoe and the wealth of the purchaser. Dog skin was highly prized for ball slippers as it was very soft and could be easily dyed to soft hues. Anyone who could afford such a luxury was "putting on the dog."

"It has sometimes seemed as if horses were as badly shod as could be; but women are even worse shod at the present day. . . . Fashionable women in this country wear a style of shoe with its elevated heel under the middle of the foot and pinched toe.

Our esteemed contemporary, the *New York Times*, says that sensible women would be very glad to wear shoes of a different pattern, but they are not to be found at the shoe stores, nor is it easy to get them made to order.

Perhaps in time it will come to walking about on stilts — which the fashionable heels of the day approach in altitude.

There is one thing about it: if girls think small calves becoming, they are sure to get them by wearing high-heeled shoes. How little women realize the draft upon their symmetry and beauty which these high heels make! If they did realize it no woman in the country would have one on a week from to-day."

Excerpt of an untitled newspaper clipping,
circa 1880s, from the scrapbook of
Nellie von Gerichten Smith

The fan was an indispensible accessory, not only because it was beautiful to look at but also because its movements had a language all their own.

By the proper use of the fan, a lady could flash a personal message across a crowded room, and those around her would be none the wiser. Carrying the fan in her left hand meant she wished to make your acquaintance, while twirling it in her left hand was the gentleman's clue to make himself scarce. One had to be very careful to read the correct message, no matter how subtly it was sent.

A lady fanning herself slowly might appear only to be overheated by the giddy mazes of the dance, but this discreet motion could also be telling a gentleman acquaintance "I am married." If she stopped fanning and held the fan in front of her face with the right hand, that was his signal to follow her. But if their little tryst was doomed to failure because someone was watching, she would subtly draw the fan across her forehead. And if she sensed she was not his first conquest, switching the fan to her right hand meant "you are too willing."

Mercedes Robles, later Mrs. Aaron Mason of Pinal County, is shown holding a fan in her right hand. Could it mean that the original recipient of this photograph was too willing? Or is the fan dropped slightly to signal that she wanted to be friends? Photograph courtesy of the Department of Library, Archives and Public Records, State of Arizona

Children's fashions often were smaller versions of adult clothing. Fortunately, fans and fancy dresses were usually saved for special occasions. The corset, however, was worn constantly by the female gender from age one or two through older age.

This photograph, taken in the mid-1870s, shows Georgia Weaver in one of the most outrageous and uncomfortable styles ever devised. Although the bustle deformed spines and displaced internal organs, it was part of every fashionable female outfit of the time, with the exception of the bathing costume (see top, circa 1890s.) The only reason it was not used as part of beach attire as well was because the bustle structure and the layers of material, decorative fringe, flowers, beading, lace, braid, feathers, and ribbons which made up the ordinary dress weighed approximately ten pounds!

Such outfits were meant to suggest the opulence of both the wearer and the father or husband who could not only provide such obviously expensive attire but also pay a servant to assist the females in the family to dress, undress, and manage the house. Anything more strenuous than draping oneself over the furniture was out of the question! Photograph courtesy of Dorothy J. Jones

In 1897 the "Buster Brown" comic strip was created by American cartoonist, Richard Felton Outcault, and out of its popularity emerged a new children's fashion. This unidentified Phoenix youngster, whose photograph was made by N. W. Mealey around the turn of the century, looks less than comfortable in his spotless white stockings, wide, lace-trimmed collar, and starched skimmer. This hat style was — in its adult version — also called a sennit, boater, or sailor, and was originally created in hard straw by Lord Horatio Nelson for use by the British Navy beginning in 1797, the same year he was commissioned rear admiral. It was revived again in America as a summer fashion for adults in the 1920s.

Short pants were worn by young male children from about the age of five, and their advancing years up to adolescence were marked by the lengthening of their trousers and a shifting similarity from the female frilliness to more masculine, and conservative, attire. Another accessory of the "Buster Brown" style which made a comeback was the black and white, spat-style saddle shoes which became a favorite of a new generation of style-conscious teenagers in the late 1940s to middle 1950s. Photograph courtesy of Sharlot Hall Museum

By the middle 1890s the gathered drapery of the
dress front and sleeve began to elaborate the female
bodice—just as the newspaper cartoon had feared—
and this shift in style served notice that the frilly,
silly lass of earlier decades was about to be replaced
by a full-figured, confident woman. No one doubted
for a moment that American women could be
consummately fashionable, but the mere suggestion
that the female form had some natural curves all its
own was a revolutionary departure from everything
that had been held true up to that time.

    With the first few years of the new century came an increase in detail and decoration of both the
bodice and hemline. The most stylish skirts featured pleats, ruffles, or other frills below the knee, and
both day and evening wear swept the ground. This elegant outfit, worn by Pearl Weaver Wilson, dates to
about 1904 — the pouched sleeve being at its zenith then. Her hair is carefully smoothed over pads to
give the coiffure enough width to display such an elaborate hat. Even this accessory began to reflect the
changing tastes and aspirations of women. The Dake Opera House on West Gurley noted in its
programs of entertainment that women would be allowed to remove their hats while on the premises
because of "these modern, reform days."

    Pearl Wilson dressed fashionably because she had the means to do so and the vivacious personality
to carry it off. But in her case, it was not only an indication of her husband's social and financial
prominence in the community. To her contemporaries there was another, more subtle, message. After all,
her husband was Joseph W. Wilson, owner of one of the finest clothing stores in Prescott! Photograph
courtesy of Dorothy J. Jones

The nineteenth century lady, in order to appear fashionable and represent her husband as doing well, was required to own suitable attire for a wide variety of activities. She needed gowns to wear while dressing, gowns for afternoon visits or teas, ball gowns, gowns for dinners, gowns to accommodate a game of lawn tennis or a carriage ride, gowns for travel, gowns for vacations, gowns for weddings, confirmations, baptisms, burials, and mourning. And heaven help the poor thing that had to bear the humiliating experience of ever wearing the same outfit more than once!

Even informal family outings, like this one, required the proper dress, hat, and cape, and this particular group had a special responsibility to appear fashionably dressed. Anthony A. "Tony" Johns (left) was the head salesman in the mercantile house of Kelly and Stephens, one of Prescott's earliest and finest outlets for family attire. Shown also are his sister-in-law, Georgia Weaver Aitken; his wife, Cora Weaver Johns; and another sister-in-law, Pearl Weaver Wilson.

While Georgia is wearing a popular hat of the 1880s and 1890s, trimmed with ostrich feathers, lace net, and velvet ribbon, Cora and Pearl sport the newest style of the late 1890s. A fashion item reprinted in a local newspaper entitled "Points Are In High Favor" advised that the very latest fad was "hats with upper tending peaks at each side . . . ." Of course, no one needed to tell the ladies of Prescott because by the end of 1898, this style — patterned after the head gear issued Arizona "Rough Riders" — was being worn by both sexes. Although they were called the "Bucky O'Neill" hat in memory of the death of Prescott's war hero, this jaunty style also celebrated the national pride generated by what newspapers of the day called that "Glorious Little War." Photograph courtesy of the Department of Library, Archives and Public Records, State of Arizona

162

Frances Lillian Willard Munds (shown here) came to the Verde Valley with her newly-widowed mother in 1879. Her father, Joel Willard, had hoped that living in the Arizona Territory would improve his health, but while traveling from Nevada with several of his sons he died enroute.

The Willard brothers ran cattle with William Madison Munds, after whom Munds Park in the Mongollon mountain range is named. Frances passed her teachers exam, and in the next several years she taught in a number of remote communities throughout the Yavapai County, including being one of the first teachers at Mayer. While riding with her brothers, she met Mund's son, John Lee, and they fell in love. On March 5, 1890 they were married by Reverend Adolphus Windes.

John Lee Munds served as a deputy under Sheriff George C. Ruffner from 1894 to 1897, and in 1898 was elected sheriff of Yavapai County. The Fall of 1898 was also an important time for "Fannie" Munds; she was elected secretary of the Arizona Woman Suffrage Organization. During the next fifteen years she worked tirelessly for this cause, never losing faith even when both houses of the legislature passed a suffrage bill in 1903, and then Governor Brodie vetoed it. Finally, on November 5, 1912 women were given the right to vote in Arizona — eight years before the U.S. Constitution was amended to allow woman suffrage. Frances Munds was appointed by Governor Hunt as Arizona's representative to the International Woman Suffrage Alliance in Budapest, Hungary, in June 1913.

Women like Fannie, who were attending college, establishing careers outside the home, and traveling unchaperoned, were less likely to feel pressured into wearing an uncomfortable, even unbecoming — yet fashionable — style and instead chose less cumbersome materials designed in a less constricting (and, some said, less feminine) manner. Women's desire for more freedom in their personal and social activities was reflected in their choice of attire. One of the few clothing items which seemed to bridge the gap between taffetas and tweeds was the ostrich feather craze.

In August 1887 the first ostriches arrived at Phoenix farms set up for the purpose of collecting and selling the luxurious feathers of these ungainly birds. The Salt River Valley supplied a large percentage of the wing and tail feathers demanded by style-conscious women in both America and Europe. Hats, like the one Frances Munds is wearing, were the most popular way to display the feathers, which had been dyed every color of the rainbow to coordinate or contrast with each outfit. For more prestigious occasions, ostrich feather boas and even fans were also highly prized accessories.

In 1914, about the same time that the popularity of ostrich-feather-festooned attire began to wane, Frances Willard Munds was elected the first female state senator in Arizona and the second in the nation. Photograph courtesy of the Department of Library, Archives and Public Records, State of Arizona

Thelma Tinsley (Booth) lived with her family at Houston, near the Tonto Basin, when this photograph was taken about 1903. One of her most precious possessions — and perhaps her only playmate — was the dog by her side.

Marian and Wilbur Webb also lived in the Tonto Basin, so called because the Apache Indians who continued fighting the soldiers and pioneers were called fools, or "tontos," by their brothers. The Webb home, Greenback Ranch, was located west of Punkin Center. There were no other children their age for miles around, Marian Webb (Armer) Schmidt recalls, so they entertained themselves by "building water wheels in the creek, playing 'farm' with animals carved from squash and cucumbers and making burros out of sticks which Wilbur outfitted with pack saddles he fashioned from Prince Albert cans."

In the March 1, 1925 issue of the Arizona Daily Star, Henry Fountain Ashurst reminisced about the ranch south of Williams where his family settled in 1876 when he was two years old:

"I motored to the old Ashurst Ranch whither I had not been for 26 years. I pointed out to H_____ many spots amongst the rocks and trees where we had played and wandered nearly 40 years ago. . . . Entering the cabin I saw the same huge fireplace before whose hearth of large, flat stones my brothers Thomas and Andrew were born and on which my sister Margaret had died. . . . The family lived on the ranch every summer from 1878 to 1890 and from 1883 to 1887 we wintered there. I found the crevice wherein my father hid our supplies when the Indians galloped along on the warpath, burning and murdering as they went on their raids. I showed my nephew the cave where my father hid mother and myself as the savages passed by on that dreadful day when the power of hope was lost. In winter the isolation of the ranch was so complete that no wanderer ever came that lonely route from October to May." Photograph courtesy of Sharlot Hall Museum

164

Child's Play

If the experiences of women on the Arizona frontier have been overlooked, the children have been all but forgotten. Few youngsters recorded the events of their everyday lives and those who lived in remote areas of the territory were often born and buried without public acknowledgement of any kind. In this day of prenatal care, childhood immunizations, and public schooling, we tend to forget that in the early days, arriving at adulthood was a considerable accomplishment in itself.

Arizona's children were given the awesome responsibility of carrying forth the dreams of their parents who pioneered this wilderness. It was they who observed and remembered the rigors of life as it had ebbed and flowed around them. And what they remembered were not the dangers or the privations —there was no sense of sadness for what life had lacked — but rather they shared a sense of adventure and pride in the lessons learned as they and the new territory grew up together.

The family shown here lived at Palomas in the Palomas mining district, eighty-two miles northeast of present-day Yuma. The area was named after flocks of white winged doves found there during the summer months. The settlement was first called Doanville for John Doan, a pioneer resident, and a post office was established on November 22, 1889. On April 18, 1891 the town's name was changed to Palomas, the Spanish word for "doves." This family dwelling is particularly interesting because it shows the mixture of Indian-Spanish/Mexican-Anglo which predominated the lifestyle of southern Arizona. The house is built of milled lumber and topped by a shingle roof with a thatched ramada added to the front, probably to provide some shade and reduce temperatures inside.

    Wagons stand ready to the side of the house, and an older child turns to wave over his shoulder while the subjects of this photograph pose for the camera. After other members of the family went off to daily chores or away to school, mother was often the only companion for those still too young to go along. Photograph courtesy of the Department of Library, Archives and Public Records, State of Arizona

Before the skills of a medical doctor were readily available to area residents, Anna Shaw served as Globe's midwife. She was relied upon for her knowledge of remedies and basic home care and was accorded the title of "doctor" because of her devotion to the needs of those placed in her hands.

    This Fourth of July float was sponsored by Doctor Anna (shown holding the reins) and represents both her patriotism and the results of her skills as a midwife. Photograph courtesy of the Department of Library, Archives and Public Records, State of Arizona

167

Doctor John R. Walls was born in Canada in December 1867. On April 1, 1896 he became a naturalized citizen in Denver, Colorado, and several years later he arrived in Prescott, Arizona Territory, with his wife, Alza.

In August 1899 Dr. Walls was one of several founding members of the Western Club, a social and athletic organization which met monthly. Dances were held for the amusement of the members and their wives, but playing cards for money and drinking alcoholic beverages were forbidden. By November members had decided to disband.

When the 1900 census was taken, Walls had an office at 114 West Gurley, and their daughter Helen was eight months old. The January 14, 1901 Arizona Journal-Miner reported that "Dr. John R. Walls has commenced his new residence on Mt. Vernon Ave." On September 14 the Walls family moved in. Here, Dr. Walls also treated his patients, and he is said to have had one of the first X-ray machines in the territory.

This photograph, taken in 1902, shows Dr. John Walls playing with his daughters, Mary (left) and Helen. The following year, Walls deeded the house to Alza and left for Tucson where he set up a medical practice on North Stone. In the 1913 Tucson City Directory, Catherine P. Walls is listed as his spouse. Photograph courtesy of Sharlot Hall Museum

The "Visit of the Magi" was reenacted over and over again in the Arizona Territory. The scene might be set on the hot desert sands of July or in a cold March drizzle in the high country, and the wise men looked more like weather-worn prospectors and trail-hardened cowboys who had traveled many miles over rough terrain to bring a gold nugget or hand-carved toy to a child they didn't know.

News of the birth of a baby spread quickly in town, although it might be several months before word reached remote mining claims and line camps. In the isolation and privation of their daily lives, a baby seemed to represent the love and security of family life which they had once known and left behind. Looking into the sweet face of Vivian Johns Baehr (shown here), born on October 13, 1899, to Edith Josephine Weaver Baehr and Rudolph Baehr of Prescott, it is understandable that such toddlers were considered the true wealth of the territory. Photograph courtesy of Dorthy J. Jones

Johnny A. Hovey, son of Sheriff and Mrs. Hovey of Graham County, was born in Clifton on June 17, 1889. He is wearing the long, full dress which was typical attire for toddlers a century ago. The rocking horse may have been a favorite toy or a prop which the photographer retrieved after the photo session, but the bowl of food looks to be all Johnny's idea. Photograph courtesy of Sharlot Hall Museum

Sand Table for Children

"A sand table is a great educator for children and furnishes them with unlimited amusement. Simply make a small low table from packing boxes, with crossed legs, sawhorse fashion, at each end, and two braces, one either side of the legs at the place where they cross, to hold them firmly in place. There should be a little, narrow rim nailed around the top of the table to keep in the sand. Now provide a keg of clean, dry sand and a little sand shovel, and the children will do the rest.

"With the aid of a sand table children can get a much clearer idea of geography than by oral description. What wonderful mountains, lakes, river courses, valleys, etc. can be made! Or, the sand may be laid out to represent a park, using bits of evergreen twigs for trees and shrubs. A real good farm can be laid out, with bits of sticks or toothpicks for fences, and toy cattle may be turned out to graze in the pastures.

Children will amuse themselves for hours with such material, gaining at the same time a certain dexterity for fashioning things that is certain to be of value to them later in life.''

—From the 1880s scrapbook of
Nellie G. Smith

Apple Roly Poly

Yield: 8 servings

1 ¾ cup sifted flour
4 teaspoons baking powder
   (not double acting)
1 teaspoon salt
1½ tablespoons sugar
4 tablespoons butter

¾ cup heavy cream
1 egg white
5 to 6 large raw apples, sliced,
   or any other fruit filling
1 cup brown sugar
Cinnamon or nutmeg to taste

Make a light, short biscuit crust by blending flour, baking powder, salt, sugar, butter and cream. Roll thin on a floured board. Brush with the white of one egg, then spread thickly with slices of raw apple, sprinkle with brown sugar, flavor with cinnamon or nutmeg, or use any other fruit filling. Roll up.

Method I

Wring a cloth out of hot water, and flour it; tie the pudding in it, allowing space for it to swell. Boil for an hour (longer if apples are slow cookers), and serve with hot molasses poured over.

Method II

Bake the roll in a greased loaf pan at about 400 degrees F. for 30 to 40 minutes. Serve with cream.

Note: This is also excellent with mince meat filling.

Dime Ginger Bread

1 ounce (1 rounded tablespoon)
 butter — costs 2 cents
½ pint of molasses — costs
 5 cents
1 level teaspoon each ground
 cloves, cinnamon, and ginger—
costs 1 cent
1 level teaspoon soda
½ pint boiling water
½ pound (2 cups) flour —
 costs 2 cents

Melt butter, add it to molasses and spices. Dissolve soda in boiling water. Mix with the molasses and lightly stir in flour. Line a cake pan with buttered paper. Pour in the batter which will be very thin and bake it for about ½ hour or until you can run a broom splint into it and withdraw it clean. The cake which will be good size will cost about 10 cents.

—From the 1880s scrapbook of
Nellie G. Smith

Old Fashioned Gingerbread Men
(Adapted)

Yield: About 2 dozen cookies

1 cup packed brown sugar
1¼ cups molasses
3 eggs
1 cup butter, at room
 temperature
1 tablespoon baking soda
1 teaspoon salt
1 teaspoon each ground allspice,
 ground cinnamon, ground
 cloves, and ground ginger
8 to 9 cups flour, divided

In a large bowl with mixer at low speed, beat brown sugar, molasses, eggs, butter, baking soda, salt, spices, and 3 cups flour until just mixed, constantly scraping bowl with rubber spatula. Increase speed to medium and beat 2 minutes, occasionally scraping bowl with the spatula. With a wooden spoon, stir in 5 to 6 cups flour to make a stiff dough. Divide dough in half and wrap with plastic wrap. Use dough immediately or refrigerate to use within 2 days.

Preheat oven to 350 degrees F. On a lightly floured surface, with a lightly floured rolling pin, roll half of dough ⅛-inch thick. With an 8-inch long gingerbread man cookie cutter, cut as many cookies as possible.

Using a pancake turner, carefully arrange cookies on lightly buttered cookie sheets. Bake 12 minutes or until edges of cookies are firm; immediately loosen cookies from the sheet and remove them to cool on wire racks. Repeat with remaining dough and re-roll scraps. Use Ornamental Cookie Frosting and raisins to decorate cookies.

Ornamental Cookie Frosting

3 ¾ cups confectioners' sugar
¼ teaspoon cream of tartar
3 egg whites

In a small bowl with mixer at low speed beat confectioners' sugar, cream of tartar, and egg whites until just mixed. Increase speed to high and beat until mixture is so stiff that a knife drawn through the mixture leaves a clean-cut path. Spoon frosting into a pastry bag with a small writing tip.

— Viola Koenig, Home Economist
Yavapai County Extension Office of
the University of Arizona

Sweet Rocks

Yield: about 5 dozen

1 cup sugar
1 cup brown sugar
1 cup (2 sticks) butter,
　at room temperature
3 eggs, lightly beaten
1 teaspoon ground cloves
1 teaspoon cinnamon

1 teaspoon baking soda
2 tablespoons water
2½ cups sifted flour
1 pound dates or raisins,
　seeded and chopped
1½ pounds broken walnuts

Beat to a cream sugar, brown sugar, and butter. Add eggs, cloves, cinnamon, soda dissolved in water, flour, dates or raisins, and the walnuts. Drop the batter in small lumps on buttered baking pans and bake in a moderately hot oven until golden brown, about 12 to 15 minutes.

Cream Whistles

Yield: about 5 dozen

½ pound (1 cup) sugar
½ cup (1 stick) butter,
   at room temperature

6 eggs, separated
Sifted flour, as needed
Confectioners' sugar

Stir sugar and butter to a cream. Add eggs, whites and yolks beaten separately, with sifted flour to make a stiff batter. Drop the mixture by the large spoonful onto buttered paper on a board or the bottom of an inverted dripping pan. The mixture should be dropped several inches apart so that the cakes can spread out thin. Bake until a light brown. It will not take more than 5 minutes. Then slip off onto a molding board that has confectioners' sugar dusted on it. Have ready a round stick about the dimensions of an old-fashioned willow whistle and roll the cakes about it while warm. When cakes are nearly cold, slip off the stick and fill with thick jelly or whipped and sweetened cream.

Vada and Alice Stringfield (whose descendants still live in the Prescott area) had their photograph taken with a girls' best friend. The wax or china heads of European-made dolls gave them a delicate reality while their cloth, wooden, or leather bodies were covered with fashionable dresses, some replicas of the latest court costumes. Although dolls made in France, Germany, England, Italy, and Holland were considered the highest quality, by the 1860s America had cornered the doll market with a new process called vulcanizing. These dolls of hard rubber were much more durable for the younger set, who soon could choose among dolls that could sit upright, move their arms and legs, drink and wet, cry, smile, and sleep.

Lois Boblett mentioned her daughter's doll in her journal:

"One day they [Charles and Isabel] went out to the wagon close by to play and Bell had her doll with her. Some way she dropped it on a rock, as there were many, and broke it all to pieces. They both screamed and we tho't the Indians had crept on them. Mr. Boblett grabbed his gun and I followed him expecting to see them being dragged off by the Indians. When we got out and found out what was the matter, we both sat down and cried and laughed together."

Such a loss was a disaster indeed to a child with no other playmate and no hope of replacing her broken companion until next time the family traveled the fifty miles into Prescott. Photograph courtesy of Sharlot Hall Museum

175

As settlements grew into towns, the diversions available to children increased. Margaret Storey (Mayes), left, and Mildred Storey (Baller) were born in Prescott exactly two years, two months, two weeks, and two days apart. This photograph, taken about 1907, shows the sisters with their twin wicker carriages and twin "teddy" bears (named after President Teddy Roosevelt).

"Margie" and "Mil" also had a variety of pet animals, including chickens, a goat, a huge St. Barnard named "Buster," and a burro brought home one day by their father Harry. The burro was a family favorite until the day he broke loose and wandered down to Whiskey Row where saloon patrons got him drunk.

Harry Storey was telegraph superintendent for the Santa Fe railroad and had an extension line connected to their house on Sheldon Street, near Pleasant (only a few blocks from where the sisters live today). They learned Morse code by watching their father work, and one day the girls decided to send a secret message, so one of them tapped out H-E-L-L. Every key on the line picked it up!

Yes, life could be pretty exciting if you knew how to make your own fun. Photograph courtesy of Sharlot Hall Museum

Family dinners were more leisurely a century ago and provided a time to discuss the events of the day. Sunday dinner was served after church, usually about 1 p.m. Chicken or turkey (steamed, not roasted which made the meat coarse) was a favorite, with the gizzard reserved for the males as it was a generally believed tale that it would make adolescent female bosoms grow larger.

No matter what the main dish was, at the Brinkmeyer's house family members and dinner guests all hoped dessert would be Ina's Wellesley Fudge Cake. In fact, this cake was so popular that Henry Jr. had the recipe adapted so it could be made and sold at the Brinkmeyer Bakery.

Shown in this photograph, circa 1902, are (left to right) Henry Brinkmeyer, Caroline (who still lives in the family house), Henry Jr., and Marcella. Mother, Ina Muzik Brinkmeyer, is standing behind Henry Jr.

After Sunday dinner, families often took a carriage ride. Sometimes the children went to Baumann's Candy and Ice Cream Factory or to Shumate's ice cream parlour. Caroline Brinkmeyer remembers that Shumates was "just this side of the Palace," and she and other children delighted in watching the Salvation Army attempt to convert patrons as they came out of the saloon. Photograph courtesy of Caroline Brinkmeyer

177

Wellesley Fudge Cake

Yield: 3 large layers or 1 deep pan about 8-by-12

1½ cups sugar
½ cup butter or shortening
  (not oil)
3 eggs
1 flat teaspoon soda or
  baking powder
½ cup hot water
2 squares melted unsweetened
  chocolate

1 cup or more sour milk,
  buttermilk, or cold water
3 scant cups flour
1 teaspoon salt (if shortening is
  used instead of butter)
1 teaspoon vanilla extract
1 cup cut up walnut meats
  (floured)

Cream sugar and shortening. Beat in one egg at a time. Dissolve soda in hot water. Mix in melted chocolate (chocolate will foam when added). Add sour milk alternately with sifted flour, add salt, vanilla and floured walnuts. Bake about 40 minutes in moderate oven. Put 2 or 3 inches above heat in oven.

Frosting

Butter size of a walnut
2 squares unsweetened melted
  chocolate

½ cup sugar
¾ cup condensed milk
1 teaspoon vanilla extract

Melt together butter and chocolate and add sugar. Stir thoroughly. Add milk and vanilla and cook to soft boil stage. Beat until cool enough to spread.

—Contributed by
Caroline Brinkmeyer

Youngsters throughout the territory enjoyed having fun together, and the larger the town, the more amusements it had to offer. Caroline Brinkmeyer and her friends rented burros from Joe Dougherty's OK Stables for twenty-five cents a day. This provided transportation to Thumb Butte for an impromptu picnic.

Granite Dells was another popular place, and you could ride out on the train for a day of picnicking, swimming, and fun. Other entertainments included birthday parties, baseball games, ice cream socials, and special community occasions such as July Fourth, Labor Day, Halloween, and Christmas.

Of course, any day was a good time to play hide and seek, three legged race, snap the whip, kick the can, potato sack race, and run sheep run. Even hiking was an enjoyable pastime, especially with the group formed by the Episcopal minister who dispensed candy along the way.

This Sunday school picnic took place about 1898 at Judge Howard's on Goose Flats. Shown, left to right, are: (back row) Mary Wright; Rose Coughlin; Doan Merrill; the fiddler, Joe Curr; Bessie Hatz; unidentified; Stanley Winds; Jessie Sanford; Violet Hatz; Inez Raible; Ella Baker; Daisy Randle; Myla Cartmel; Hattie Crane; Eva McCandless; Irene Martin; Judge Howard, with white beard; Robert Connell, Sr.; (front row) _____ Winds; unidentified; Julius Rodenberg; Earl Sanford; Beatrice Connell; Winifred Connell; Gladys Wright; Ethel Shull; Gussie Raible; Beryl Robinson; Gideon Shull; Charlie Herndon. The woman standing in the doorway is Fannie Stevens who gave the first music lessons in Prescott and was one of the town's earliest school teachers. Photograph courtesy of Sharlot Hall Museum

The rigors of territorial life were borne in equal share by the children, who were expected to help as soon as they were old enough. They filled the wood bin or coal buckets, carried water, fed the animals, weeded the garden, picked wild berries, washed dishes and did other kitchen chores, and often watched the younger children.

Often adult emigrants saw only the primitive living conditions, moral depravity, wild animals, and lonely, barren landscape. The desert sand was infested with fleas; clothing and bed covers were at times invaded by centipedes, tarantulas, lizards, snakes, and scorpions; the isolation was complete and the work never ending. Yet, children who were born here or came to Arizona at an early age enjoyed a freedom not known to city children. They were healthier and learned not only to adjust to their circumstances but to enjoy the independence they had.

This unidentified young couple found good hunting in the Cave Creek area about a hundred years ago. Like many other frontier women, this girl rides a western saddle, instead of the less practical and more pretentious side saddle which ladies "back in the States" were required by custom to ride. *Photograph courtesy of the Department of Library, Archives, and Public Records, State of Arizona*

A number of towns in the territory, as well as organizations such as the Phoenix Indian School, sponsored baseball teams, and competition was keen. This photograph, taken in 1907, shows the Yuma Baseball Club members (front row, left to right) N. S. Parks, outfield and team captain; _____ Godfrey, second base; _____ Smith; team mascot, _____ Durmax; Dan Maddox, outfield; Julius Levy, scorekeeper; (standing) Larry O. Neil, first base; _____ Nagle, pitcher; _____ Hogan, third base; Bob Bechtel, team manager; _____ Nelson, catcher; _____ Whalen, short stop; _____ Nelson; L. F. Lewis.

Being a player on a community baseball team — especially a winning one — was very prestigious, but "team mascot" was an honor accorded only a few lucky young men. *Photograph courtesy of the Department of Library, Archives and Public Records, State of Arizona*

180

PRESCOTT HIGH SCHOOL ROOTERS

These unidentified young ladies, whose photograph was taken about 1908, cheered on the Prescott High School football team at the municipal field on East Gurley where they played all games. This unimproved acreage made for an exciting rough-and-tumble game played with plenty of enthusiasm from both team members and their pretty classmates who shouted encouragement from the sidelines. Photograph from the collection of Myrtle Stephens, courtesy of John Hays

181

In 1880 George Whitwell Parsons noted in his journal that Tombstone was the fastest growing city between St. Louis, (Missouri) and San Francisco, (California). Thirty-one years later, when this photograph was taken, Tombstone was no longer a rowdy boom town populated by silver seekers, gun slingers, and Jezebels whose only desire was to strike it rich. Those who stayed on wanted to be part of a substantial community in which to raise their families.

Records indicate that the first Boy Scout troop in the territory was established in Tombstone sometime during 1911 by Scout Master Matthew Telin. Sharlot Hall of Prescott, the Territorial Historian, was chosen as "lady of the troop." This photograph of the founding members was taken in front of the office of the Tombstone Prospector and includes (left to right, back row) Scout Master Matthew Telin; Allen Corbett; Gilbert Hanley; unidentified; Rowland York; Les Hill; Ernest Davis. (Front row) Arthur Lamb; unidentified; Bud Land; unidentified; unidentified; Howard Benedict; Walter Lamb, Wallace Corbett; and the flag bearer, Phillip Rockfellow. Photograph courtesy of Sharlot Hall Museum

Shumate's was the place to go in Prescott, no matter what your age. Harry Shumate created delightful and delicious concoctions in his ice cream parlour on Montezuma Street. Sodas sold for ten cents, phosphates were fifteen cents, and customers could sip them leisurely at the little tables with decorative wire-back chairs in the front of the shop. Here, many a beau treated his best girl, and once Dora Rosenblatt Heap treated about thirty playmates, saying "charge it to my Papa." Dora recalls that this particular event was never repeated, at least not by her.

The large glass jars lining the wall just past the soda fountain were filled with a colorful array of penny candies, including gum drops, red hots, jelly beans, licorice, and jaw breakers.

In addition to the ice cream parlour, shown here in 1903, Harry Shumate ran an ice cream concession at Granite Dells during the summer months and also had a catering business. Photograph courtesy of Sharlot Hall Museum

Taffy

1 cup dark brown sugar
1 cup brown Karo (or ¾ cup
   Karo and ¼ cup molasses)

1 tablespoon lemon juice
2 tablespoons butter

Thoroughly mix all ingredients and then cook quickly without stirring until brittle when a small sample is dropped into cold water (about 275 to 300 degrees F. on a candy thermometer.) Pour mixture into a buttered pan and cool until it can be handled. Turn in the candy from the edges to form a large lump and pull it with the hands — moistened with ice water or butter to keep it from sticking. The longer the taffy is pulled the better it will taste, and the texture should be light and porous. Roll the taffy into long strips and cut it into pieces about 1 inch square. Wrap each piece in waxed paper; if stored in a tightly covered container, the candy will stay creamy and chewy instead of hardening.

— Dora Rosenblatt Heap

A buggy ride was one of the most common pastimes of young adults a century ago. Shown in the front seat of this rig are (left) Gayle Allen and (right) Charlie Herndon, and in the back seat are Hattie Fisher and Mulford Winsor.

Josephine Stephens notes in her diary a number of the activities she participated in prior to her marriage to Warren C. Potts on February 7, 1883:

April 6, 1879 — Joe and me went to get violets down in the creek.

April 10 — Price came down at night   went to the Calico Ball   had a good time.

August 1 — Went by [Sam] Millers for a little while started back home and met H. M. Huebert and had a race.

August 7 — We went for a ride   met eight or nine buggies while we were out.

August 30 — J. Marks wanted to have a trotting race with him   we did and beat him.

December 25 — Price and H. Rice came down and we took a slay (sic) ride   then we went in the country to a dance.

Even in those days, young ladies wished to have some say about whom they "kept company" with, and attempts at match making were not appreciated — at least not by Josephine. She wrote on March 20, 1879: "Old Gosper [Secretary of the territory but considered by many the true governor because Fremont was away from Arizona so much of the time] came down and took lunch with us today the old fool I hate him."

Picnics, band concerts, theatrical productions, social calls, and holiday activities also provided suitable entertainment. Leona J. Gray of Tempe, daughter of Hortense Frankenburg Jones, remembers outdoor games such as "Last Couple Out," box suppers, and taffy pulls being very popular pastimes as well. Photograph courtesy of Sharlot Hall Museum

Chocolate Carmels

2 cups molasses
1 cup brown sugar
1 cup heavy cream
½ pound chocolate, broken into

small pieces
Butter, the size of an egg
2 teaspoons vanilla extract

Except for vanilla beat all ingredients together. Boil until it thickens when dropped in cold water. Stir in vanilla and then turn into buttered tins. When nearly cold, cut into squares or diamonds.

Fudge

2 cups sugar
¼ cake unsweetened chocolate, melted

1 cup rich milk
1 tablespoon butter
1 teaspoon vanilla extract

Boil sugar, chocolate, and milk together in a heavy saucepan or double boiler until the syrup forms a soft ball when tested in cold water. When this stage is reached, add the butter and vanilla extract, then remove from heat. Beat the syrup hard until it begins to thicken and is creamy in consistency, but not sticky. Quickly pour into buttered tins and set aside to cool. Cut into squares when the fudge has set.

The college girl made this candy popular, sometimes cooking it over the gaslight fixture after "lights out" in the dormitory.

Keeping a diary has been a way of recording innermost feelings for countless individuals, and in its pages are detailed aspects of everyday life never reported in newspapers, magazines, or other publications of the day. Such is the case with the diaries of Alice Olivia Butterfield shown here in 1894, at age sixteen. Ten years later, in 1904, she began her journal entries.

Alice noted that she was five foot, ten inches tall; weighed 144 pounds; wore a size 6¼ glove and size ten hose; was fluent in French (which she lapsed into for her more intimate entries); rode a Pierce bicycle; played Flinch, Bridge, and golf; and lived at 509 East Adams in Phoenix. At that time, postage was two cents an ounce, a shampoo and set cost fifty cents, and chocolate sundaes were sold two for thirty cents. A 1901 graduate of Stanford University, Alice arrived in Tucson on Monday, January 4, 1904 to teach history at the University of Arizona, which had been established in 1885 to appease the town for the loss of the territorial capital. Her salary as a college instructor was seventy-five dollars monthly.

"Saturday, January 9, 1904 — Had quite a long talk with W. Jones, drat folks anyhow, I wish they would mind their own business. I am not engaged to anyone.

"Monday, April 18 — We four had glass of beer and spent evening discussing events.

Wednesday, October 2 — Saw 'Candida' at Hardwick Theater Tuesday (tickets seventy-five cents). Had another weepy fit. Bothered nerves anyhow or blues. Guess my liver is out of whack.

"**Sunday, January 1, 1905** — *Last year T.P., this year Mr. D., who next. Mr. Diehl took Nat [Alice's girlfriend] and I driving to hieroglyphics and he is beginning to declare himself. I'm afraid I was bad. The very Old Nick gets into me. I will try to be more careful. Had him to dinner and played piano after for him.*

"**Tuesday, January 3 —**

There was a young lady of Siam
Who said to her lover named Priam,
If you kiss me, of course,
You will have to use force
But my dear, you are stronger than I am.

"**Thursday, January 26** — *At capitol in p.m. to help decorate governor and executive department [for] reception to legislators and judges of Supreme Court in governor's office. Have received and entertained guests. My silver used for dressing table.*

"**Friday, January 27** — *Judge Wells of Prescott has consented to take governorship so Frank [Alice's step-father] does not have to.*"

Note: Frank W. Nichols came to the territory in 1880, settling first in Tombstone and the following year relocating to Willcox, where he served as Justice of the Peace for sixteen years. He later moved to Phoenix when appointed Territorial Auditor, was acting governor during Governor Brady's term of office and later served as secretary of the territory.)

"**Thursday, February 9** — *Well, Frank will probably have to take governorship after all and Mr. Paige is scheduled for his place. That keeps us poor — I wonder if it will go through.*

"**Friday, February 10** — *Compromise candidate — Judge Kibbey's name sent to Senate by President.*

"**Monday, February 27** — *Entertained at dinner the Tritles, McCarty and the Paiges. Menu — iced grapefruit punch, cream of celery soup, oysters and macaroni and cheese, roasted peas, salad, carmel ice cream.*

"**Sunday, March 5** — *Had a quiet day at home. Phone has been out of whack all day — hence peace.*

"**Tuesday, March 7** — *Went to Capitol to see Judge Kibbey installed as governor. Sat on floor of office. Oath administered by Chief Justice Kent in office.*

"**Sunday, March 12** — *Mr. and Mrs. Clark, Anderson and Looney of Yavapai County gave a picnic at Echo Canyon, Camels Back. Dr. Bristol and Mr. Davis attentive not especially, but nice. Dr. B. rode home with me and walked to house. Invited him to dinner and spent the eve. I like him.*

"**Sunday, March 19** — *Went driving with Mr. Diehl. Oh dear, I wish I was as sure of my own mind as he was but does he really care for me or just want his home again and could I care for him and do I want to. He tried my braiser (sic) and when I wouldn't let him laughed such an amused satisfied laugh as if to say, alright I'll wait.*

"**Tuesday, March 28** — *To races and driving with Mr. R. Deering. Nice boy and will be good looking someday when his skin clears.*

"**Sunday, April 2** — *Driving with Mr. Diehl — had a perfectly delightful time. I muchly fear I am going to succumb.*

"**Tuesday, April 18** — *Served scrambled eggs and mushrooms in chafing dish. Mr. D. staid (sic) ¾ of an hour after the rest had gone and I did not like it. I wish he would not do things that look so settled. Gertrude would sure think now that we are engaged. I wonder if we will be. I do not think so.*

"**Monday, July 17** — *Mama is right — I do not care for boys anymore.*

"**____, September 28** — *Met a Mr. Hewins. Nice man.*

"**Saturday, December 30** — *Mr. Hewins took me to Fair races. I like him even if he is a bit older than I.*

"**Friday, January 5, 1906** — *Divine Science class. Mr. Hewins to call — if in town. I like him. Called   spent eve and brought me Kodak views.*

"**Wednesday, January 10** — *To the theater with Mr. Hewins. I do like him immensely. He invited me to go horseback riding some day next week. Letter from Dick Dooner. Shall I answer it?*

"**Thursday, January 11** — *Tried to get dinner but not understanding use of stove as well as gas did not succeed. Anyway, I can make biscuit.*

186

"**Saturday, January 27** — *Had nice phone chat with Mr. H. I wonder why I like him. Do I like him any better than any one else. I wonder.*
"**Monday, January 29** — *Frank thinks the Statehood Bill will go through. Oh, dear and I don't want to go to Los Angeles or to teaching next year either.*
"**Wednesday, January 31** — *Mrs. Brewer gives party in eve. Go with C. Cornell. Mr. D. there and was as devoted with eyes and manner as I gave him opportunity to be.*
"**Thursday, February 15** — *In eve Mr. Hewins called and stayed quite awhile. He continues interesting. Asked me to chaperone him to Miss Ellis kindergarten.*
"**Sunday, March 11** — *Carl Hayden and Jack Hamlin called this afternoon. I am glad to have met Mr. Hayden as I have heard of him so often. He seems very nice. Wish I could really get to know him but I doubt I would really like him.*

"**Tuesday, May 22** — *Mr. Hewins called in eve. Wonder why I feel like telling him all I know.*
"**Wednesday, June 6** — *Driving [with] Mr. Bradley in eve. If only I cared to flirt but I do not care much about it I guess. Anyhow, when he waxes complimentary, voice changes becomes musical and he gets tiresome.*
"**Thursday, June 7** — *To Park Theater with Mr. Hewins. Oh dear, what has struck the men-folk anyhow.*
"**Friday, August 17** — *To reception at the Cunninghams in eve. Mrs. Davies heard in Tacoma that Will H. had never married because he was so in love with me. Fancy!*
"**Sunday, December 23** — *Driving with Mr. Hewins and his cousins, Mr. and Mrs. Lee Adams. Anyhow, it grows stronger and stronger and I just like to be near him. I do not believe he realizes how much I care. I never felt so toward anyone before. John slightly but not quite like this. Oh, I hope we can and that he still cares as he knows me better. He is strong and good.*"

As the territory emerged a new, progressive state, its brightest prospects were reflected in the intelligent, energetic generation epitomized by Alice Olivia Butterfield. She was a strong, sensitive woman rubbing shoulders with great personalities and historic events . . .but what became of her "Mr. Hewins"?

187

Holidays and
Special Occasions

There was much to celebrate in the Arizona Territory, despite — or perhaps because of — the difficulties of everyday life. Each culture, ethnic group, and family unit had its own unique traditions and noteworthy events, but the fun of a party was understood by all and knew no nationality.

Social gatherings also provided a "head count" of sorts in the early days, a way to keep up with who had been born, gotten married, been killed, or had just given up and moved on. There was a justifiable pride in the homes and livelihoods these pioneers had wrested from the wilderness, and it was a natural tendency to want to share this joy of accomplishment with others who appreciated how hard won were such cultural refinements and how great were their importance to the progressive development of the territory.

Moreover, every marriage performed, every Independence Day celebrated, every Christmas carol sung was a link with loved ones left behind and a reaffirmation that their dreams and the territory they believed in would endure.

Alma Mary Harris and Merton W. Stewart (shown here) were married in 1907. The bride's mother, Mary Ellen Sears Harris, came to the territory with her family in April 1880 when she was twelve years old. She was one of the first thirty-one students to enter the Territorial Normal School (now Arizona State University) in Tempe when it opened in 1886. Alma also attended Tempe Normal and taught school until her marriage.

The groom had arrived in the Salt River Valley, where his family took up farming, in 1893 when he was nine years old. After marrying Alma, they moved to his cattle ranch southeast of Mayer.

Their daughter, Ellen Stewart Hardin, tells what living on the Stewart spread was like for her parents: "It was a pioneer's life in those early days at the ranch. All travel was by horseback except going to town in the wagon. Though my father was very good to help with the heavy work and was an excellent cook when there were cowboys or summer visitors to be fed, it was still a hard life for the woman of the house. My mother learned to shoot a rifle, enough to take a hawk on the wing if it threatened the chickens, or trail a bobcat from the hen house.

"My parents were instrumental in getting a one room country school for the neighboring ranch children. On Sundays, my mother gathered the children together for bible study.

"The ranch was a focal point for many a bar-b-que for friends and relatives. The family often drove in the wagon to dances and other social events." Photograph courtesy of Ellen Stewart Hardin

Stack Cake

On the frontier, Stack Cake was the traditional wedding cake. Each guest brought a thin layer as his gift to the newlyweds, who could often measure their popularity by the height of the cake.

Yield: three thin layers, 10 to 12 servings

2 cups flour
½ teaspoon salt
½ teaspoon baking soda
½ cup butter, at room
    temperature

½ cup sugar
½ cup molasses
2 eggs
½ cup milk
About 2 cups of applesauce

Sift together the dry ingredients and set aside. Cream the butter, sugar, molasses, eggs (one at a time), and milk, alternating with the dry ingredients. Mix well and pour about ½-inch deep into three greased 8-inch layer pans. Bake at 375 degrees F. for about twenty minutes or until cake springs back to the touch. Cool the layers about 10 minutes, then remove from pans and let cool several hours before assembling. Spread applesauce between each of the three layers.

Stack cake can be topped with whipped cream and nuts, or to add a unique touch, a lace doily can be placed on top and sprinkled with confectioners' sugar. Remove doily carefully so pattern remains distinct.

Note: Cake layers were traditionally held together using spicy applesauce. If sugar is not available or you prefer not to use it, raisins can be added to the applesauce to add sweetness. Fortunately, cooks of today do not have to remove raisins from their stems or seed them before using.

"All notices of marriage where no bridecake is sent, will be set up in small type and poked in an outlandish corner of the paper. Where a handsome piece of cake is sent, it will be put conspicuously in large letters. When gloves or other bride favors are added, a piece of illustrative poetry will be given in addition. When, however, the editor attends at the ceremony in person and kisses the bride, it will have especial notice — very large type, and the most appropriate poetry that can be begged, borrowed, or stolen." —From the 1880s scrapbook of Nellie von Gerichten Smith

From the *Phoenix Gazette* of Thursday, July 18, 1907.

"The wedding of Miss Alice Olivia Butterfield and Mr. Levi Edwin Hewins last night at the home of Secretary and Mrs. W. F. Nichols, 509 E. Adams, was one of the most brilliant affairs seen here in some time. Though the wedding was a rather quiet affair, only a few of the most intimate friends of the contracting parties being present, tasteful and wonderful decorations made the scene one of rare and entrancing beauty.

"The color scheme in the library, where the ceremony was performed, was green and white. Potted plants of vivid green were interspersed with snow white oleander blossoms.

"At 9:30 o'clock the bridal party entered the rooms to the strains of Lohengrin's Wedding March rendered by Mr. Frank D. Lane. Miss Drew Bennett, as bridesmaid, led, and next came the bride, accompanied by Secretary Nichols. The bride's dress was a wonderful creation of pineapple gauze, trimmed with pearl passementerie. Rev. Harold Govette and the bridegroom, accompanied by Dr. Ancil Martin, met the party.

"The ceremony was very impressive, and after the friends of the newly united couple had showered their congratulations the company repaired to the reception room. George H. Smith, the gardener of the capitol grounds, had transformed the large screen porch in the rear into a refreshment room of surprising beauty. The large room was walled in by banks of potted plants in endless variety, a particularly imposing corner being devoted to a weeping cabbage palm in bloom, used probably for the first time in Arizona, for decorative purposes. Over all was a gorgeous illumination of Chinese lanterns that cast a mellow glow over the festive scene. But the particular feature was the pleasing suggestiveness of the table decorations. The centerpiece was a large vase of American Beauty roses and the white linen was almost hidden from view by the ornamentation of greenery, each stem and flower selected with the thought in mind of its special significance and the occasion of its use. For instance, the bride's seat, which was designated by a bow of white ribbon, was at a corner made verdant by a profusion of sweet myrtle, emblematic of love, while the next corner, reserved for the groom, was decorated with laurus noblis and the palm flowers of victory.

"The presents tendered were displayed in another apartment, and were numerous, beautiful and costly. The offerings embraced almost everything that could be conceived of as suitable for such an occasion and all were just what they should be, entirely suitable. There was silverware of the finest kind, engraved and in many instances with special designs suggested by the occasion, as orange blossoms, some in single pieces and much of it in entire sets and chests, China ware and Japanese ware, of the most handsome sort, as well as linens in quantity, drawn work, lamps, valuable brasses, quantities of cut glass, old English glass ware, no longer found in the markets, chafing dish, coffee sets, etc. a multiplicity of things that will be cherished to the end."

191

Helen Mary Wells (left) was the daughter of Judge Edmund W. Wells and Rosalind Banghart Wells, who both came to Chino Valley in 1864. This is Helen's wedding picture and also shows Emma Dutcher, who served as her attendant. Emma's father, Doctor Egbert William Dutcher, was a popular local physician who had died in September 24, 1898 from injuries received while attempting to rescue two women from a burning house on North Pleasant.

The groom was Harry William Heap, who had come to Phoenix in 1896 as secretary for the trolley system — then called the Phoenix Railway Company — and for the Phoenix Water Company. In 1898 he was made general manager of both companies, and the following year — on October 5, 1899 — he and Helen were married in the home her parents had built in 1879 on the southeast corner of Cortez and Carelton streets.

192

Judge and Mrs. Wells spared no expense to make their daughter's marriage a beautiful and memorable occasion. They arranged for Madame Potts of San Francisco to design the bridal and bridesmaid gowns, and flowers were shipped by train from San Francisco to decorate the entrance hall, refreshment room and this intimate wedding chamber — complete with two satin pillows for the couple to kneel on and an arrow-pierced heart overhead. Photograph of Helen Wells Heap courtesy of Sharlot Hall Museum. Photograph of Wells house interior courtesy of Dora Rosenblatt Heap

Angeline Brigham Mitchell, always called Angie, was an organist at the Westside Church in Prescott and the first teacher at the West Prescott school (now Miller Valley School). This tintype was made of her in the spring of 1874.

The Daily (Prescott) Arizona Democrat *noted her marriage to the Honorable George E. Brown on April 20, 1881 in the following manner:*

BROWN-MITCHELL — *At the residence of Mrs. A. B. Mitchell, West Prescott, on the 20th instant, by Rev. Mr. Hunt, Hon. George E. Brown and Miss Angie B. Mitchell.*

So our friend Brown has become a bridegroom, a much more reputable position than that of a Republican member of the Legislature! He has married, too, one of Prescott's most accomplished and agreeable young ladies. The happy couple left town immediately after the ceremony for Mr. Brown's ranch on the Agua Fria. Long life and happiness to both!

The Democrat *office acknowledges a present of excellent wedding cake, for which, individually, and collectively, it returns thanks.*

Independence Day was an important occasion throughout the territory and in Prescott it was celebrated in a variety of ways. People by the buggy load came in from the mining claims and ranches to stay for several days. Everyone — especially the ladies — wore stunning new outfits, one for the daytime events and even fancier attire for the evening ball. The formal ceremony on the Plaza included patriotic music and recitations, speeches by politicians, and the reading of the entire Declaration of Independence — in both English and Spanish. Other activities during the day included a community barbeque or picnic on the Plaza, games and contests for all ages, and the discharging of firearms and small explosive charges.

Beginning in 1881 a group of local businessmen organized the "Horribles" and entertained the populace with a parade from their clubhouse on McCormick Street to the Plaza, followed by a band concert. It is not known whether their name was based on their appearance or their instrumental endeavors, but their activities were source of much merry amusement.

Shown in this photograph, taken on July 4, 1891, are left to right — Joseph Roberts as the policeman; A. A. Emanuel as an old woman with a man on her back; Crook Marion (son of John H. Marion) as a Roman soldier; Adolph Moser as a fat Dutchman with a pipe; A. C. and Robert Burmister as an elephant with J. A. Tobin a Nubian keeper; Joseph Tiernan as a lost child with a rattle; and H. D. Derwin as an immense bottle reading "the only thing that sustains Prescott is good American whiskey." Other participants are unidentified. Photograph courtesy of Sharlot Hall Museum

Independence Cake

½ cup (1 stick) butter, at
   room temperature
2 cups sugar
2½ cups flour
2 heaping teaspoonfuls
   baking powder
⅓ teaspoon salt

1 cup milk
5 egg whites, stiffly beaten
Cochineal or red food
   coloring
Blueberries or blue food
   coloring

Cream butter with sugar. Sift together flour, baking powder, and salt. Then add alternately milk and flour mixture. Beat hard for three minutes, then stir in stiffly-whipped whites of eggs. Make one layer white, another colored red with cochineal (this was made from the dried bodies of female cochineal beetles, but use red food coloring), and another blue with blueberries. Bake in 3 layers at 350 degrees F. for 30 minutes or until cake tests done. When cold put together with white frosting and decorate the top with red, white, and blue frosting, and a small flag stuck in the center.

Excerpt from an oration delivered on Independence Day, July 4, 1866, by Governor Richard C. McCormick.

"The day on which we meet, ever dear to the American pioneer, seems doubly glorious, as we contemplate the return of national unity and peace.

"The pioneer is seldom a politician. With the cunning arts of policy he has little sympathy, while demagogism is his abhorence. As a true patriot, however, he has an interest in the welfare of his country, and his views of public matters are broad and generous. To others he allows the wildest liberty of opinion and action, consistent with an honorable fidelity to the laws; and he condemns no man for not thinking as he thinks.

"While the progress of the pioneer upon the Pacific slope was not absolutely retarded by the [Civil] war; and it will ever be a glory of the Republic that in the heat of the contest new Territories and States were here organized, and peacefully and prosperously controlled; the restoration of public tranquility and the increased stability of free institutions, will give a new stimulus to pioneer enterprise, and must prove greatly advantageous to our immediate public and private interests.

"If its [territorial] resources are such as we believe them to be, the day is not distant when it will be occupied by a large and thriving population —when the iron horse [railroad] will prance through its hills, and over its plains; and the lightning [telegraph] afford instant communication with all parts of the continent. Capital and labor will assert their potent sway; art will vie with nature in providing attractive homes, and luxury will take the place of want.

"But to give full effect to the work of the pioneer we must look beyond gold and self, to the highest interests of the commonwealth. As good citizens it is our duty to see that law and order keep pace with the material development of the country; that society is carefully organized; that justice is upheld, that virtue is respected and that truth, freedom and patriotism prevail. In no other way can we so well honor the memory of the men who have yielded their lives...or do justice to the pioneers who survive and watch, with unfeigned pride, the growth and success of the country of their choice."

Another exciting event which took place during the Fourth of July was the competition between the four companies of the volunteer fire department. The object of the 100 yard footrace was to see which team could be the first to lay hose and pump water through it. Here Company No. 4, the "Toughs," are shown racing the clock down Gurley Street to a finishing line in front of the Journal-Miner office. Although Company 4 was the champion hose cart team of Arizona, New Mexico, Texas, and California in 1890, 1891, and 1892, the Toughs failed to get the pipe fixed to the hose and William Bayless led the "Dudes" to victory.

One memorable Fourth of July, about 1907, Gail Gardner remembers seeing a balloon ascension from the Plaza each day of the celebration. The hot air balloon had a trapeze suspended underneath, and seated on the bar was a person of the female persuasion. For each of her three ascents she wore a different costume — one red, one white, and one blue — with a spangled bodice, brief ballet skirt, and TIGHTS. In those days of long, leg-hiding skirts, the spectacle of a lady in tights was enough to guarantee a crowd, and the youngsters (of which Gail was one) and menfolk seemed particularly fascinated by this lovely little lass because she knew some brand new "cuss" words! Photograph courtesy of the Department of Library, Archives and Public Records, State of Arizona

Chinese emigrants became an important part of the economy throughout the territory, but instead of being admired for being industrious and having strong family and religious ties, their desire to retain their own cultural identity was not understood and their customs, dress, and the long braid worn by the men were publicly ridiculed. Nevertheless, the Chinese continued to make efforts at living peacefully with others and, despite the fact that they were denied citizenship in many states, they had strong patriotic feelings not only for their native land but also for the country which had given them the opportunity to prosper. Here a group of Chinese adults participate in a parade held in Phoenix about 1900. Photograph courtesy of Sharlot Hall Museum

Hallowe'en Salad

Yield: 4 to 6 servings

1 head cauliflower
Lettuce leaves as needed
A few beets
Thin mayonnaise, or

dressing made from equal
measures of oil and
vinegar
Salt and white pepper

After soaking cauliflower, head downward, in salted water for an hour, tie it in a cheese cloth and cook till tender in salted, boiling water. When cool, separate the flowerets carefully and dice the stalks, laying them over fine curly lettuce leaves. Have a few deep-red beets cooked tender; carefully cut them in slices and remove the inner layers to make rings. With a small pastry cutter cut one or two beets into heart shapes, dispose the hearts and rings over the flowerets, and when ready to serve cover with mayonnaise or dressing, seasoned with salt and white pepper.

This group of Prescott residents is ready to attend a masquerade party held sometime in 1882. Carrie Johnson Aitken (far left) is the only identified participant. Photograph courtesy of Sharlot Hall Museum

Halloween was not a children's event in the early days of the territory. There were not many youngsters in Prescott, and those who were here were not allowed to leave the safety of the cabin after dark. But the young, unmarried adults often threw caution to the winds. In 1867 a Halloween social was held at the Prescott House on Granite Creek. A report in the *Arizona Weekly Miner* commented: "Esquire Blair assures us that there were a thousand young ladies present and everyone of them altogether lovely. Making due allowances for the Squire's nerves, we conclude that the array of female loveliness was particularly brilliant, so that the boys felt like good Methodist brethren at a camp meeting — it is good for us to be here."

Mrs. General George Crook (as local newspapers called Mary Dailey Crook) starred in a play entitled "Trying It On" in 1873, at Fort Whipple. Dancing followed until midnight when a buffet was served. The billiard room was usually where such suppers were held, the entire billiards table being piled high with goodies of every description. One local newspaper described the scene: "The table was adorned with a centrepiece forming a Chinese pagoda containing a revolving Chinese lantern, and laden with roast pigs, turkeys, chickens, salads, jellies, etc."

By the mid-1870s masquerade parties were not only held at Halloween but throughout the year, as well. The February 2, 1877 edition of the *Arizona Miner* printed the following item in their gossip column, entitled "Local Intelligence."

"Mrs. Kelly, the enterprising dress-maker a few doors north of the Miner office, has sent to California for quite a large number of masks to meet the demands of all who may wish them for the coming Washington's Birthday Masquerade Ball."

Josephine Stephens (shown here) attended a masquerade party as a "Jockey" on February 22, 1878. Her costume theme is denoted by the jockey's cap worn saucily on the back of her head and the riding crop in her left hand. The mask was usually worn during the masquerade ball until the midnight supper. Another masquerade party, held on March 11, 1878 was, according to the Miner, "without exaggeration or doubt, the grandest affair of the kind ever gotten up in this Territory. About one hundred and fifty persons, military and civic, attended in elegant and costly costumes, assuming almost every character known. There were Kings and Queens, Princes and Princesses, and so on, down to the most humble peasant represented, and so perfect were the disguises, that husbands did not even recognize their own wives. Major Wilhelm, as 'Genii,' was a perfect disguise and caused much merriment. Lieut. Henely, as a 'Peruvian Don' would have put a Mexican vacquero to blush. Mrs. Colonel Biddle, as a 'Chinese maid,' was acknowledged the best. Mrs. W. N. Kelly in striped red and white silk dress, jewelry to correspond, white slippers, seven button kid gloves, was richly dressed. Her sister, Miss Josephine Stephens, was dressed in the same style, except color of material, and their costume (sic) acknowledged to be equal to any present. A party appeared as ghosts, and puzzled the 'congregation' somewhat as to who they were for a long time. It was ultimately discovered that they were not ghosts but genuine 'good folk' from town and named Will. C. Bashford, R. H. Burmister, A. Burmister, Coles

Bashford, Mrs. W. C. Bashford, Mrs. R. H. Burmister and Miss Lizzie Bashford, all of whom, after removing their pillow cases and white sheets, appeared in elaborate evening costumes, hardly ever surpassed anywhere.'' Photograph courtesy of Sharlot Hall Museum

Hot Spiced
Apple-Cranberry Punch

Yield: 10 servings

6 teaspoons whole cloves
6 sticks cinnamon
2 cups water

1 cup brown sugar
5 cups apple juice
4 cups cranberry juice

Tie the cloves and cinnamon in a cheesecloth bag and simmer in the water for 15 minutes. Remove the spice bag and add the brown sugar and juices. Heat to a serving temperature.

Witch Apples

Yield: 6 servings

6 large apples, cored
6 marshmallows
6 to 12 cubes sugar

12 to 18 maraschino cherries
6 tablespoons brandy

Bake apples until soft, but not long enough to burst the skin. When cooked, insert a marshmallow into the core space, put a cube or two of sugar on top and a few maraschino cherries on each apple. When ready to serve turn over each a tablespoon of brandy and light just as the table is reached. The brandy will burn with a ghostly blue flame and melt the sugar and marshmallows. Whipped cream served in a bowl is a favorite addition to the dish.

Halloween festivities were enjoyed by both children and adults in Prescott by the 1880s, and there was a wide variety of community events to choose from. The social whirl accelerated considerably in 1892. A dance was held at Lynx Creek with candidates from both political parties in conspicuous attendance, hoping to combine potlucking and politicking. Another dance benefitted the Prescott Orchestra, and an afternoon concert was given on the Plaza by the Prescott Brass Band. Ice cream socials were very popular that season, as well.

In 1894 Professor Zambach came to town. He made a Halloween appearance at Patton's Opera House and received a standing ovation for his greatest feat of legerdemain, the "Dancing Skeletons."

Brightly colored posters hailed the arrival of one of the circuses which found its way to Prescott and invited all to attend the street parade commencing its 1898 engagement. "Great Wallace Shows"

NO. 1.—SWISS WAITING-MAID   NO. 2.—TROUBADOUR   NO. 3.—MAGICIENNE

boasted a menagerie, museum, aquarium, and a Royal Roman Hippodrome featuring ten acres of canvas, seating for ten thousand people, a half-mile race track, one hundred acts, twenty-five clowns, six bands, and the most competent and beautiful ballerinas, aerialists and equestrians. It was a spectacular and long remembered event, and all who attended felt that it lived up to its billing as a "triumph of art, music and good taste." Photograph from the 1880s scrapbook of Nellie von Gerichten Smith

Preparing the Turkey

Cut the head off close, leaving the neck long. Cut through the skin around the knee joints and bend the foot backward. This draws the tendons so they can be seen. Run a skewer under them one at a time (there are 7 on each leg), and draw them out. The drumsticks will then be as tender and nice as any other part. Cut a small opening at the rump and draw out the entrails. Split the skin along the back of the neck to the body. Cut the neck off close to the body but not the skin. Remove the crop and feet, and wash inside and outside. Scald and skin the feet and cook them and the neck with the giblets. Fill the body of the turkey two-thirds full of dressing (when too full the dressing packs), and close the opening with white twine stitches. Also, put some dressing in the crop cavity and fold the long neck skin back and catch with a few stitches. Tie down the legs and wings, rub all over with warm butter, dredge heavily with flour, salt and pepper, lay in a baking pan, pour in boiling water ½ inch deep, and set in a very hot oven until the outside is lightly browned to prevent the escape of the juices. Then let the oven cool down and bake at a moderate heat 20 minutes for each pound of the turkey's weight, basting every ten or fifteen minutes.

If the giblets have been cooked the day before, add that water to the pan with the turkey. If not, place them in the pan also to cook. For the gravy, chop the giblets fine, rub 1 tablespoon butter with 3 of flour. Put the turkey in the warming oven, place the pan over the fire, add enough boiling water to make 1 quart; stir in the flour paste, boil up until thick, stirring all the browned sediment loose from the pan. Add salt and pepper, the chopped giblets and serve.—From the 1880s scrapbook of Nellie von Gerichten Smith

This hunter bagged Thanksgiving dinner in the Mongollon Rim area about 1903. Photograph courtesy of the Department of Library, Archives and Public Records, State of Arizona

Prescott did not observe Thanksgiving officially until November 29, 1866, almost three years after the territorial capital was established. The *Arizona Weekly Miner* commented: "This is the first time a day of Thanksgiving has been set apart in this Territory, but we trust it will be duly respected. While, as people we have much to contend with, we certainly have much to be thankful for, and we should be glad to introduce here a custom so pleasing and proper as that of annually acknowledging the blessings we have received and imploring a continuation of Divine favor." A traveling minister, Reverend D. M. Blake, preached at the religious service held for that first Thanksgiving.

The upcoming Thanksgiving Ball was the big news in the November 21, 1868 *Miner*:

"The ball that is to come off in Moeller's new building on Montezuma Street Thursday evening next, promises to be the biggest blow-out ever given in the Territory. Excellent music will be scratched and tooted, and the supper (Ah! that's what'll catch our ten dollar Greenback) will be superb."

The following issue, editor John Marion gave this account of the proceedings:

A nice young lady with auburn hair asked us if we would like to dance. We muttered something about awkwardness and told her we should even marry sooner than dance. We then adjourned to the pleasing prospect set before us in a glass tumbler, which we passed through our battery and down into our amalgamated works. We are neither a dancist nor the son of a dancist; nevertheless, we take great pleasure in gazing upon lovely ladies and brave men as they glide through the 'giddy mazes of the dance.' Forty little and big feminines were present, and, of course, four times as many masculines.

Governor A.P.K. Safford proclaimed November 18, 1869 as Thanksgiving Day in the territory, "although our people have been sorely scourged and afflicted during the past year and many of our bravest and best citizens have fallen beneath the scalping knife and tomahawk of our savage foe, and death and desolution has been brought to many homes." Marion attended a Thanksgiving dinner at Governor Safford's residence along with several U.S. judges and prominent business men. He reported in the November 20 issue of the *Miner*:

The spread was excellent in variety and style of getting up as any we have assisted at in Prescott. The sight of the little roasted porkers, chickens, and other fixings caused our bosom to swell and our heart to beat with emotion. Toasts and short, pithy speeches were numerous; sanguine railroad projects and death to the Apaches were the Themes of the hour. If all the hopes and predictions there expressed could be realized, we should not care to live elsewhere than here.

Cranberry Sauce

1 quart cranberries
Water to cover
About two cups sugar

About three tablespoons
  orange rind, grated

Stew cranberries in water until the berries burst open. Add sugar, draw the cooking vessel (never use tin — a porcelain pot is best) to the back of the stove and let simmer one-half hour longer. Set the cranberry sauce away to cool. As it begins to thicken, add about 3 tablespoons of orange rind, grated freshly. Serve chilled.

Corn Fritters

Yield: 4 to 6 servings

½ cup flour
1 teaspoon baking powder
¼ teaspoon salt
⅓ cup yellow cornmeal
¼ cup milk

1½ tablespoons butter,
  melted
1 to 1½ cups corn kernels
  cut from left over cobs
1 egg

Mix dry ingredients. In a separate bowl beat together the milk, butter, and egg. Add this to dry ingredients and then add corn, stirring only enough to combine. Drop a large ladleful of fritter dough into hot fat about 1-inch deep. A piece of raw potato will keep the pan from burning. You can cook 3 or 4 fritters at a time as long as they are not crowded. As soon as one side is fried a golden brown, turn it over with a perforated spoon or spatula.

Serve at once with butter on top if part of the main course or with confectioners' sugar sprinkled on top for dessert.

Pumpkin Pie

1 cup evaporated milk
1 cup dry steamed and sifted
  pumpkin (or canned)
½ cup brown sugar
2 tablespoons each of
  molasses
  and melted butter

2 raw eggs, slightly beaten
½ teaspoon salt
1 teaspoon each cinnamon,
  cloves, and ginger
1 teaspoon vanilla extract
9-inch pie shell

Mix milk, pumpkin, sugar, molasses, butter, eggs, and flavorings. Pour into a plate lined with pastry and bake at 400 to 425 degrees F. for about one hour. Cool before slicing and serving.

Pumpkin Bread

Yield: 2 loaves or 24 to 36 cupcakes

5 cups flour
6 teaspoons baking powder
3 teaspoons cloves
2 teaspoons cinnamon
½ teaspoon salt
1 large can pumpkin
2½ cups honey (1 to 1¼ cups

sugar plus ¼ cup liquid
  equivalent to each cup
  of honey)
1 cup vegetable oil
2 eggs
1 cup water
2 cups raisins (optional)

Mix all dry ingredients together. Except for raisins, add other ingredients to bowl and then mix in dry ingredients as you stir. Add raisins last after all ingredients are well mixed. Bake loaves for about 1 hour at 350 degrees F. or cupcakes at 325 degrees F. for about 20 minutes. May be eaten plain or iced with confectioners' sugar mixed with only a teaspoon or two of milk. (Evaporated milk will give it a richer flavor.)

1906 Dinner Menu

First Course —
    Oysters, canapes, cantaloupe
Second Course —
    Chicken giblet soup and consomme

Third Course —
   Columbia River Salmon
Fourth Course —
   Entrees, croquettes, sweetbreads
Fifth Course —
   Vegetables
Sixth Course —
   The joint or principal meat — Leg of Lamb, Beef Loin, Ham Loin,
   Pork Loin, Chicken, Stuffed Veal
Seventh Course —
   Frozen punch, cheese, omelette
Eighth Course —
   Suckling Pig, venison
Ninth Course —
   Salad
Tenth Course —
   Puddings, Bavarian cream
Eleventh Course —
   Ice Cream or Frozen Desserts
Twelfth Course —
   Coffee, liquors

Thanksgiving dinner on November 24, 1910, at Poland Junction. Seated left to right are:
   George Duff, Florence Jones, Cam Jones, Dr. C. R. Keith Swetnam, Mata Dexter, C. J. Dixon,
and Bert Leonard.
   Mata Eliza Dexter arrived in Prescott in 1905 to accept a teaching position and went on to become
principal of Washington School, principal of Lincoln School, and an influential member of a number of
social and civic organizations. Dexter School is named after her. Photograph courtesy of Sharlot Hall
Museum

Lion Coffee — roasted and packed by Woolson Spice Company of Toledo, Ohio, and Kansas City, Missouri — was very popular with customers, and in every pound package was a beautiful trading card for the kiddies to add to their collections. During the year, children's storybook characters were featured so the little tykes would be sure Mommy bought the right brand of coffee. This card was specially designed as a giveaway for the Christmas season. Photograph courtesy of Sharlot Hall Museum

Snowballs

Fried cakes, it would seem, are primarily a man's dainty, women, as a rule, caring little for them. However, since we must make them, we want them attractive enough to tempt any palate, and the fact of a fried cake pleasing a feminine appetite is accepted as proof unfailing of its perfection. A perfect fried cake is not only toothsome, it is as dainty in appearance as the finest loaf or layer cake. It does not suggest fat either to the eye or the stomach and may be eaten from gloved fingers, if desired, without danger of soiling.

Yield: 2½ to 3 dozen

2 eggs, thoroughly beaten
1 cup sugar
3 level tablespoons melted butter
1 cup sweet milk

2 teaspoons baking powder
Flour as needed, only enough to
allow the dough to be rolled
out on the board for cutting.

Combine eggs, sugar and melted butter, and milk. Sift together baking powder and flour. Add to the egg mixture. Up to this stage, the mixing should be done with the spoon, and the dough handled with the fingers as little as possible.

To shape them appropriate to their name, the dough should be rolled a good ½ inch thick, and cut out — not with the common doughnut cutter, but with an ordinary sized wine glass. From the center of these cut smaller circles with a silver thimble. This may seem a mistake, since it is desired to have the cakes spherical, but the vent is really necessary to perfect cooking. Without them the cake is likely to be soggy, and does not cook evenly. Fry in deep, hot fat to a delicate brown and drain on crumpled white or brown paper, which will absorb any superfluous fat. When nearly cold, roll in confectioners' sugar until thickly coated; if done when the cakes are warm the sugar will form a sticky coating.

When done, the cakes will be perfect spheres with no visible opening in the center, and with their thick coat of sugar will much resemble their namesake, both in appearance and in the rapidity with which they will disappear.

When Governor John Noble Goodwin and his official party left Leavenworth, Kansas for the western wilderness in September 1863, they expected to be at Fort Whipple in time to celebrate Christmas and the establishment of the territorial capital simultaneously. As it turned out, rough terrain, danger, delays, accidents on the trail, and many other difficulties hampered progress towards their intended destination, and Christmas Eve found the territorial officials miles away from their goal, suffering from the bitter cold and stinging snow.

Protected only by the wagons pulled around in a tight circle to buffer the intensity of the winter gale, these newcomers to the wilds of Arizona warmed themselves with a large bonfire, cheerful camaraderie, and a huge cauldron of steaming hot toddy. Stirring speeches were delivered, but the speakers' exaggerated motions were more for the purpose of keeping warm than rousing a response from the audience.

Entertainment was provided by hand-clapping, foot-stomping, and what few musical instruments were brought on the journey by members of the governor's party. High-spirited choruses of "John Brown's Soul," "Limber Dick," and many other popular songs of the day echoed off the surrounding mountains as Christmas "cheer" warmed both body and soul. The festivities ended with a simple but eloquent invocation by the chaplain, asking that Providence be with them as they attempted to establish a territorial capital in the middle of the wilderness.

Christmas 1864 was celebrated in the recently completed governor's residence. A short service of song and prayer was followed by a buffet dinner cooked by Henry William Fleury, private secretary to Governor Goodwin. By 1865 Margaret Hunt McCormick had joined her husband, Governor Richard Cunningham McCormick, and it was she who suggested and assisted with the first Christmas tree to grace the parlor of the log "mansion." Grandmother Ehle (who had the only sewing machine) and other women of the community had spent the fall months making little gifts for the children, and they were presented to them at the governor's home, a custom which continued for a number of years.

John Marion reported in the pages of the *Miner* that during the children's Christmas party at the official residence in 1868 "many grown persons were affected almost to tears while listening to Miss Louisa Zaff and her little brother, Johnny, singing the plaintive song, 'Father Come Home.'" Marion also attended Christmas dinner at the home of Mrs. J. P. Bourke:

"We, along with several crusty bachs [bachelors], partook of an excellent meal. It was by far the best dinner we have ever sat down to in Arizona and we had thought it impossible for a lady to procure and prepare so many good things in so new a country."

Christmas dinner wasn't the only tasty gift Marion received that year. In the personals column of his January 2, 1869 edition he announced that:

"Raible and Schearer of the Pacific Brewery, next door to the *Miner* offices on Montezuma Street, gave us, as a Christmas present, a keg of lager, for which they have our thanks. The keg is getting along as well as can be expected considering the lager has long since 'evaporated.'"

The 1869 holiday season was ushered in with a performance by the Roth Dramatic Company, composed of soldiers from Fort Whipple. The Christmas ball was described for readers in the December 12 issue of the *Miner*:

The coming ball promises to be a stunning affair. A floor is being laid in Moeller's splendid hall; the walls thereof will be splendidly decorated; the music, the best on the continent of Arizona, will be in attendance; no loafers, rowdies, or disreputable persons of either sex will be admitted. And to crown all, the supper which will be served at Hagan's restaurant, will be superior to any thus far devoured in this town.

The editor of the Enterprise reminisced in a December 1876 issue:

"Who is there among us for whom the return of Christmas brings no bright memories? Do we not all recollect ourselves as little rosy urchins waking up at early dawn and tip-toe peeping into the little stocking to discover the goodies that dear old Santa Claus had sent us? The good cheer, the deluge of toys and 'goodies,' the bright glow of the blazing Yule log that glared from the hearth and brought a sparkle into a dozen little eyes that watched the 'faces in the fire,' all these are gracious memories. The earnestness with which we ran and stumbled through the mazes of 'blindman's buff,' or scrambled for victory in the game of hunt the slipper! All these things come back to us and photograph the scenes of a happy childhood upon the scroll of memory. We think with pleasure of the time when we intrepidly, and yet with some misgivings, kissed the little neighbor girl under the mistletoe, and how relieved we were to find that she didn't seem to be the least bit mad about it. We recollect with gratitude the old Christmas Tree and the glorious fruit it bore. We see once again the grand, gloomy old church in its holiday dress of garlands and evergreens. And as our mind reviews these happy memories, we feel grateful for the return of the glad season that shed so much brightness on our young life."

These unidentified children enjoyed Christmas at St. David, circa 1890s. Photograph courtesy of The Arizona Historical Society

Bartolomeo "John" Belluzzi was born in Italy and went to sea at an early age. On a voyage to San Francisco, he developed phlebitis and rather than submit to amputation, he and a friend jumped ship.

John worked his way to Globe where he found a job in the newly-opened Old Dominion mine. In a local newspaper, he read that land was open for homesteading in the Mongollon Rim area. Choosing a spot on the map, he set

213

out to find the place where his dream — land of his own — would be fulfilled. Along the upper East Verde River, Bartolomeo Belluzzi claimed his parcel of land and began homesteading in 1874. It later became known as Whispering Pines Ranch, and many of his descendants still live in the area.

One of his granddaughters, Margaret Murphy, relates that Grandfather Belluzzi's house became the center of family celebrations. "With four cousins, and assorted aunts and uncles, the log and adobe house was full. On Christmas Eve, we children were told that if we sat quietly in the living room, we'd hear Santa coming. In the quiet, on a clear moonlight night, sleigh bells could be heard as Santa approached. Almost afraid to breathe, we listened as he quieted his reindeer, stomped the snow from his feet, grabbed up his bag and made his entrance. What a glorious memory!"

A close knit family, the Beluzzi clan gathered to share special occasions and wedges of Potato Cake baked by Ira's mother and aunts.

Potato Cake

⅔ cup butter or shortening,
  at room temperature
2 cups sugar
4 eggs, separated
2 to 2½ cups flour
3½ teaspoons baking powder
½ teaspoon salt (if
  shortening is used in place
  of butter
½ teaspoon each nutmeg,

cinnamon, allspice, and cloves
1 cup mashed potatoes
  (about 3 medium potatoes)
2 squares chocolate, melted
  or 5 tablespoons cocoa
½ cup milk
1 teaspoon vanilla extract
1 cup chopped nuts
  (walnuts, almonds or whatever)

Cream the butter and sugar, adding the egg yolks one at a time. Sift together 3 times the flour, baking powder, salt and spices. Add potatoes, chocolate, and flour mixture, alternating with the milk so it will mix together easily. Add vanilla. Beat the egg whites until stiff, fold in the nuts and add this to the cake batter. Pour into a greased loaf pan and cook in a moderate oven (325-350 degrees F.) for about 1 hour or until golden brown and springy to the touch.

Papa Rosenblatt's Fruit Cake

"Papa" — Paul Gherhardt Rosenblatt — came to Prescott in 1892 and was superintendent of the metal shop for Samuel Hill Hardware Company. This was an old family recipe made back in Tennessee by his mother and brought to this country from Ireland by her.

The fruit cake was prepared long before Thanksgiving and thereafter it was aged by sprinkling brandy over it twice a week up until Christmas time. I managed to keep my fingers licked clean while helping Papa until Mama — Dora Cordelia Leach Rosenblatt — decided I was taking rather long naps afterwards.

The ingredients are approximate as the recipe was in Papa's head:

1 pound cream butter
1 pound brown sugar
1 cup dark molasses
1 dozen eggs
1 teaspoon each cloves, cinnamon, allspice, nutmeg (mixed in ⅓ cup red wine)
1 cup orange marmalade
3 pounds seedless raisins (floured)
2 pounds golden bleached raisins

(he used Sultanas)
1 pound currants
3¼ pound citron (fruit mix)
1 cup canned pineapple
1 pound blanched, split almonds
4 to 5 pounds flour
1 small teaspoon baking soda (mixed in 3 teaspoons cool water)
1 teaspoon vanilla extract
1 teaspoon almond extract

Mix butter, sugar, molasses, eggs. Add flour, spices, soda and water, and extracts and combine well. Stir the raisins, currants, citron, pineapple, and almonds in; then pour the mixture into several heavy pans about 20 inches square, which have been buttered and lightly floured. Bake at 275 degrees F. for 4 to 5 hours or until a broom straw inserted in the cake comes out clean."

— Dora Rosenblatt Heap

Dora Rosenblatt Heap remembers that Santa Claus — assisted by her father — trimmed their family tree. On Christmas Eve, after she and Pauline, Bertha, Louise, Jennie, and Paul III were asleep, he arranged tiny candles on the tips of branches and hung tarlatan bags filled with nuts and hard candies all over the sweet-smelling evergreen.

After the Rosenblatt children opened their presents on Christmas morning, other youngsters in the neighborhood were invited to come calling and choose little sacks filled with goodies to take home.

This photograph, taken in the Arizona Territory sometime around the turn of the century, shows an unidentified young lady with her Christmas gifts and tree. Photograph courtesy of Arizona Historical Society — Buehman Collection

Christmas Plum Pudding

½ pound of beef suet from kidney
1 pound raisins
1 pound currants
Dry crumbs of a six-penny loaf
   of bread (about 1 pint)
1 pint of milk
1 to 2 cups flour
2 eggs

2 tablespoons brown sugar
Wineglass of brandy
Grating of one nutmeg (about
   1 teaspoon)
1 teaspoon each cloves,
   cinnamon
Pinch of salt
Other spices if desired

Sauce
¼ pound of butter
½ pound confectioners' sugar
Brandy to taste

Chop fine the beef suet. Stone and chop raisins. Wash and pick currants. Soak the dry bread crumbs in milk. The batter needs to be thicker than cake batter, so add 1 to 2 cups flour as needed. When it has taken up all milk, add raisins, currants, suet and well beaten eggs, brown sugar, brandy, nutmeg, cloves, cinnamon, salt and other spices if desired. Mix well and place in tall fruit cans and cover tops tightly with a double thickness of paraffin paper tied with string. Place in a tall kettle about ¾ full of water. Cover and steam for 4 to 4½ hours. Let set 10 to 15 minutes before removing to cooling rack.

For a sauce, beat butter to a cream with confectioners' sugar and flavor with brandy.

—From the 1880s scrapbook of
Nellie G. Smith

Alma Mary Harris Stewart's

Mince Meat

Yield: about 4 quarts

5 cups chopped cooked beef
2½ cups chopped suet
7½ cups chopped apples
3 cups cider
½ cup vinegar
1 cup molasses
5 cups sugar
¾ pound citron, chopped
2½ cups whole raisins
1½ cups chopped raisins
Salt to taste

Juice of 2 lemons and 2 oranges
1 tablespoon mace
2 teaspoons each cinnamon
  and cloves
2 nutmegs, grated
2 teaspoons lemon extract
1 teaspoon almond extract
3 cups liquor in which beef
  was cooked
1½ cups brandy

Mix ingredients in the order given, except brandy, and let simmer 1½ hours; then add brandy and shavings from the rind of the lemons and oranges. Store in sterilized jars topped with paraffin.

— Ellen Stewart Hardin

Spiced Raisin Cake

¾ cup light brown sugar
2 teaspoons cinnamon
½ teaspoon each nutmeg,
  allspice, and cloves
Pinch salt
5 tablespoons melted lard or
  shortening

3 tablespoons molasses
1 cup thick sour milk or
  sour cream
1¾ cups bread flour sifted
  with 1 level teaspoon soda
¾ cup raisins, cut in two
  and well floured

Combine sugar, cinnamon, spices, and salt with melted lard and molasses. Beat well and add sour milk or sour cream and flour-soda mixture. Continue beating and fold in raisins. Put into an ungreased pan 10-by-6-by-2 and bake in a moderate oven (325 to 400 degrees F.) for 45 minutes to an hour or until golden brown. Sprinkle sugar on top just before putting in the oven.

Eggnog

Yield: 8 to 10 servings

8 to 10 eggs, separated
Confectioners' sugar to taste
1 pint chilled whipped cream
1 quart whole milk

2 teaspoons vanilla extract
$\frac{1}{4}$ teaspoon salt
Nutmeg to taste

Beat egg yolks vigorously, then gradually add sugar. Mix in whipped cream, milk, and vanilla. Beat egg whites and salt briskly until stiff, then add to the eggnog and serve topped with nutmeg.

Arizona was admitted to the Union as a sovereign state on February 14, 1912, exactly fifty years to the day after it had been confirmed as a Confederate territory. The fight for statehood began in earnest in the 1890s and was as difficult a battle as any fought by Arizona's frontier settlers. It was a dream for which they would accept neither substitution nor compromise. Sharlot Hall wrote:

In his message of December 1905, President Roosevelt advised that Arizona and New Mexico be admitted into the Union as one state. In Arizona the opposition to the 'joint statehood' measure was bitter and determined. Coming by train from Flagstaff to the ranch, I got the papers and read the message. I grew more and more indignant as I read and after reaching the ranch I asked my mother, who thought I was coming down with pneumonia, to let me have a fire in the sitting room. I finished the poem by 11 o'clock that night and the anger had entirely cured the cold.

Going on to Phoenix, I read the poem to Frank Nichols, to know if he thought it too strong. He entirely approved of it and he and Gov. Joseph H. Kibbey had it printed as a 'broadside' and placed upon the desk of every member of both houses at Washington.

Arizona

(First of eight stanzas)

"No beggar she in the mighty hall where her bay-crowned sisters wait;
No empty-handed pleader for the right of a free-born state;
No child, with a child's insistence, demanding a gilded toy;
But a fair-browed, queenly woman, strong to create or destroy.
Wise for the need of the sons she has bred in the school where weaklings fail;
Where cunning is less than manhood, and deeds, not words avail;
With the high, unswerving purpose that measures and overcomes;
And the faith in the Farthest Vision that builded her hard-won homes."

By Sharlot Hall From *Cactus and Pine*
Reprinted with permission from
Sharlot Hall Museum

State House Stew

Yield: 6 to 8 servings

2 pounds beef stew meat,
  cut into chunks
Salt, pepper, oregano, sweet
  basil, and bay leaf to taste
Flour seasoned with salt, pepper,
and paprika to taste
6 to 8 carrots, cut in
  3- to 4-inch pieces
6 potatoes, cut into squares
2 onions, cut into quarters

Boil meat, remove scum, and season meat to taste with salt, pepper, oregano, sweet basil, and bay leaf. Simmer until tender, remove meat and bay leaf, and add vegetables to cook until tender. Drain meat and roll it in seasoned flour. Brown on all sides in hot fat. This is why men request this...crisp, tender meat with juicy vegetables. Strain the liquid in which meat was cooked through several layers of cheese cloth before adding vegetables. Serve vegetables in a bowl with the juice and the meat on a platter.

Biscuits are served with the stew, butter-baked to be firm enough to sop up the juice without becoming soggy. Melt ¼-pound butter in baking pan. Make biscuit dough firm enough to drop by spoon into melted butter, turning to coat all sides. Bake at 450 degrees F. for 12 to 15 minutes and serve hot.

— Old Ruffner family recipe and a favorite of
Sheriff George Ruffner's good friend,
Governor Benjamin Baker Moeur

Patrick O'Sullivan came to Prescott in 1894 and worked in the U.S. Land Office. Two years later, he was appointed assistant district attorney, but his sights were set still higher, and in 1908 this young, ambitious politician ran for the office of Yavapai County District Attorney. O'Sullivan had the gift of oratory, popular at the time, and the acumen to use phrases and analogies on the communication level of the audience he was speaking to.

On a campaign trip by horseback, he arrived at the Congress Mine to address about three hundred miners employed there. The rally, which only men attended, was held outside. In the finest tradition of the old-time Democrat, he censured the Republican Party before the gathering of working men as the party of big business and rich men. Finally, he placed the thesis in focus. With waving of arms and appropriate drama, he said:

"Gentlemen, if my stomach was full of epsom salts and I had croton oil up to my collar bone and castor oil up to my neck, I would no more trust the Republican Party than I would me own bowels under them circumstances!" He carried the Congress Mine, but lost the election. In 1911 Patrick O'Sullivan was finally elected as County Attorney during the first state elections.

The first Arizona senators to serve the new state were (Democrat) Marcus Aurelius Smith, a Tombstone lawyer who was first elected to Congress in 1886 and a delegate eight times between then and 1910, and (Democrat) Henry Fountain Ashurst, also a lawyer who, at thirty-eight, was one of the U.S. Senate's youngest members. Carl Trumbull Hayden, formerly (Democrat) Maricopa County Sheriff, won the only Arizona seat in the House of Representatives. At the time of Hayden's retirement in 1969, he had served seven terms in the House, seven terms in the Senate, was president Pro Tempore of that body making him third in line for the presidency of the United States, and had served longer in Congress than any other person in American history.

Although a Republican Party was formed in 1880, first holding a Yavapai County convention sponsored by the Republican Club of Prescott and then a territorial convention in Phoenix, its influence was not noticeable in Arizona's early years.

The notation on the back of this photograph reads:
"This is L to R   Dr. Looney   his sister-in-law (do not remember her name)   George Wylie Paul Hunt, Speaker of the House — later Governor of Arizona several years   yours truly   Joe Dillon. Mrs. Dillon took the picture. Dillon used to be considered political boss of Arizona and Hunt was a special friend of his. I was Hunt's clerk, picture taken in Phoenix   January 1905. [Signed]   Mrs. Davy Clifford."
Photograph courtesy of the Department of Library, Archives and Public Records, State of Arizona

George W. P. Hunt prospected in Colorado before coming to Globe in July 1881. There he waited tables, worked in the mines and drove a delivery wagon for the Old Dominion Commercial Company. In ten years time, he worked his way up to president of the company. Although Hunt had only eight years of formal education, he was the people's choice for mayor of Globe when it incorporated in 1907.

Along with his friend and political ally, Joe Dillon of Prescott, Hunt worked actively to secure the passage of the statehood bill, and he presided over the constitutional convention called in 1910 to establish a system of state government for Arizona.

Although Judge Edmund Wells of Prescott was backed by the influential Arizona Republican (still published in Phoenix), George W. P. Hunt — the Democratic contender — won the race for first governor of the state. He was reelected for a second and third term and also served as Arizona's sixth, seventh, eighth, and tenth governor.

Samuel Hill Hardware on Montezuma Street across from the Plaza was decorated for Admission Day and displayed a banner reading "Arizona The New State" above the forty-eighth star added to the flag. To the left is the office of the Prescott Courier. *Photograph courtesy of the Department of Library, Archives and Public Records, State of Arizona*

At 2:00 p.m. following the formal inauguration ceremonies and Governor Hunt's speech in Phoenix, a military parade was held, culminating with a forty-eight gun salute. The *Arizona Journal-Miner* noted:

> No formal inauguration ball is planned but an informal reception will be held at Hotel Adams to which all citizens of the newly-admitted state are invited. The recently paved Central Avenue in front of the hotel will be washed and covered with a canopy of electric lights and the public will dance thereon to the music of a brass band and a choral society of one hundred voices, following addresses from the portico. At 8:00 p.m. the world is invited to drink a toast on the admission of Arizona and the completion of the chain of states from Atlantic to Pacific.

Acknowledgements

We wish to acknowledge the following people and organizations who shared their individual and collective records, scrapbooks, letters, and reminiscences: The staff of Sharlot Hall Museum, especially Sue Abbey, archivist, and Carol Patrick; Wilma Smallwood and Carole Downey of the State Archives; Governor Bruce Babbitt; the staff of the Prescott Public Library; Claude Cline; Lucy Miller of the Yavapai Indian Tribe; Margaret Rigden and John Hays of Kirkland; Dorthy J. Jones of Tustin, California; Phil & Renee Ball of Bradshaw Mountain Photo; library and photo archives staff of the Arizona Historical Society; Judith Simpson; Viola Koenig, home economist for Yavapai County Extension Service; Joyce Osborn Avery of Redmond, Washington; Carmen Hamilton; Kay Manley; Pat Quirk, horticulturist for Desert Botanical Gardens, Phoenix; Rebecca Ruffner Tyler; Dora Rosenblatt Heap; H. L. Davisson of Walnut Creek, California; Prescott "Scott" Benson of Phoenix; Frances Claypool Boom of San Bernadino, California; Ann Meyer, executive secretary of the Coolidge Chamber of Commerce; Carol Moore, archivist, Tempe Historical Society; Barbara Schoen, president of the Casa Grande Valley Historical Society; Robert Lenon of Patagonia; Margaret Murphy of Payson; George and Robert Birchett of Tempe; Georgia Newcomer of Scottsdale; Milton Webb and Marian Webb (Armer) Schmidt of Sun City; Leona J. Gray of Tempe; Marie Peters Wells of Casa Grande; Caroline Brinkmeyer; Joyce Segner of the Mayer Library; Ellen Stewart Hardin of Tempe; Genevieve Stringfield of Prescott; Barbara Weiner, Press Assistant to Senator Dennis DeConcini; Elisabeth F. Ruffner for proofreading and offering invaluable suggestions; and special thanks to Helen Hartin, who introduced us to Nellie von Gerichten Smith's scrapbooks, and Marguerite Noble, who shared encouragement, suggestions, and friendship.

With their assistance, photographs, recipes, home-remedies and other incidences of territorial life are individually reproduced here as authentically and completely as is humanly possible.

Bibliography

Public Collections

Sharlot Hall Museum Archives. Photographs, diaries, personal, and public records.

Department of Archives, Library, and Public Records, State of Arizona. Photographs, diaries, and personal, and public records.

Prescott Public Library. Reference materials.

Phoenix Public Library. Collection of J. H. McClintock, personal papers.

Arizona Historical Society, Tucson. General research information and photographs.

Cooperative Extension Service, Yavapai County.

Tempe Historical Society. General information and area contacts.

The Casa Grande Valley Historical Society. General information, area contacts, and photograph.

Private Collections

Myrtle Stephens Collection. Martina Kelly scrapbook, Josephine Stephens diary, general information, and photographs provided by John Hays.

The Osborn/Avery Collection. Geneological records of the Osborn family and general information.

Ruffner-Weiner Collection. Photographs, personal papers, and scrapbooks of Nellie von Gerichten Smith.

Weaver/Baehr/Jones Collection. Geneological records of the Weaver, Baehr, Kelly, Johns, Stephens, and Wilson families, general information, and photographs provided by Dorthy J. Jones.

Books

Arizona Territory Post Offices and Postmasters (1961), by John and Lillian Theobald, Arizona Historical Foundation, Phoenix.

The History of Tonto (1976). Edited by Al LeCount — A Bicentennial project by the Punkin Center Homemakers.

The Territorial Architecture of Prescott, Az. (1978). Compiled and edited by Billy G. Garrett for Yavapai Heritage Foundation.

Victorian Fashions and Costumes from Harper's Bazaar 1867 to 1898 (1974). Edited by Stella Blum Dover Publications, Inc. New York.

Webster's New International Dictionary — 2nd edition (1941). Unabridged. G and C Merriam Co., Publishers Springfield, Mass.

Who's Who In Arizona — Vol. 1 (1913). Compiled and published by J. Conners, President of *The Arizona Daily Star,* Tucson, Az.

225

Pamphlets

Informational pamphlet from Montezuma Castle, courtesy of the National Park Service.

Informational pamphlet from Palace Station, courtesy of the Prescott National Forest.

Unpublished, untitled narrative used for "Big Bug Stomp" celebrating Mayer, Arizona's 100th anniversary — compiled by Ione Johansen.

Other Sources

Coolidge Chamber of Commerce. General information and area contacts.

Casa Grande Chamber of Commerce. General information and area contacts.

Desert Botanical Gardens, Phoenix.

Payson Chamber of Commerce. General information and area contacts.

Tempe Chamber of Commerce. General information and area contacts.

Index

228